Science of Parenthood's

The Bigger Book of
Parenting
Tweets

Featuring more of the
most hilarious
parents on Twitter

Kate Hall and Science of Parenthood

SCIENCE OF PARENTHOOD PRESS

Library of Congress Control Number: 2015905208

ISBN-13: 978-0-9962262-0-2

Edited by Kate Hall, Norine Dworkin-McDaniel and Jessica Ziegler

Design and Cover by Jessica Ziegler

Science of Parenthood books are available at a special discount when purchased in bulk for premiums and sale promotion as well as for fundraising or educational use. Special editions or book excerpts also can be created to specification.

For details, contact info@scienceofparenthood.com.

Science of Parenthood Press
342 Lake Amberleigh Dr. Winter Garden Fl 34787
scienceofparenthood.com

Printed in the United States of America
First printing April 2015

To everyone who has ever laughed at
one of our jokes.

Now look what you've done.

Contents

Foreword

by Farah Miller and Emma Mustich
Editors of HuffPost Parents

Hello, our names are Farah and Emma, and we read a lot of parenting content.

Recently, we came across a blog post we loved—a personal essay with a strong message—but both of us had a feeling we'd read a piece on the same topic before. What was it? An article on another site? Part of a book? An email? Something we actually published? We couldn't remember, and Google wasn't helping at all. Finally, it dawned on us that the "essay" we both thought we'd read was a tweet. From two years ago.

In our memories, a thought conveyed in fewer than 140 characters had taken on all the gravity and coherence of a fully developed argument. Perhaps this is just another sign of how short our attention spans are. Or, maybe, that tweet's brief—and funny!— observation was more than enough to get our brains turning on the topic at hand.

Really, it was no surprise to either of us that a tweet had staying power.

For the past two years, we've been rounding up twenty to thirty of them each week for our Funniest Parenting Tweets series. We have strict requirements for the tweets that make it into a collection.

They must:
1. Be funny
2. Be about parenting
3. Have been tweeted that week

We never have a shortage of great material. And it has become one of the most popular features on our site.

Like the longer-form essays we publish every day, these tweets are lifelines: proof that other moms and dads have had the same crazy thoughts and experiences with their children.

Which is why we were so excited when Science of Parenthood and Kate Hall teamed up to publish *The Big Book of Parenting Tweets*. Portable lifelines! And now, it's time to devour the second installment, which will take you through a full year of life with kids. You may think you're just reading pages filled with jokes, but we have a feeling these words will stick with you for many parenting seasons to come.

Farah Miller and Emma Mustich
The Huffington Post

Introduction

To everything—turn, turn, turn—there is a season—turn, turn, turn. — The Byrds

If you're like most parents we know, you probably spend most of your time saying:

Turn off the lights!
Turn down the volume!
Did you turn in your homework???
OMG! Turn off the computer!

That's parenting. Day in. Day out. Year after year. No matter what the season—though perhaps more so in spring, summer, fall and winter—huh—guess that's every season. Well, the point is, parenting is fun *and* hard, the same *and* different, all the time. It's an unfortunate truism that children WILL spend eighty percent more time arguing about homework than actually doing it. Children WILL repeat every unfortunate thing you say at the most inopportune moment. Children WILL barf, hork and crap on you—occasionally all at once. And your life, your living room, your minivan ... will all be in shambles. At least for a while.

Fortunately, there's great camaraderie among those of us who are suffering through these same indignities. And even greater laughter to be shared when someone deftly sums up those universal frustrations in 140 characters or less.

In our first book, *The Big Book of Parenting Tweets*, we invited thirty-four of the funniest Twitter comedians ever to diaper a baby to hit us with their best tweets. And we could barely stop laughing to edit that book.

This time, we wanted to go—surprise!—

BIGGER! So we opened submissions to the entire Twitterverse and netted another twenty top-shelf jokesters who had us snorting and laughing even more. We suspected that some of the tweets that left us rolling had hilarious backstories that didn't quite fit into 140 characters. So we gave those tweeps a bit more latitude to answer the question, *Where the hell did THAT come from?* You'll find those little gems, called The Story Behind the Tweet, scattered throughout the book.

More tweets. More hilarity. That's our goal. Read 'em and weep! With laughter, of course.

Disclaimer: If you are Twitter stickler you may notice that some of these tweets go over 140 characters. Editorially, we took some minor liberties, adding correct punctuation and italicization for movie or book titles, for example, to aid in readability offline. Settle down.

PART 1

The Promise of Spring

Behold the joys of spring! The days get warmer. The sun shines longer. The daffodils burst forth from the garden. We can venture out of the house without worrying that another eighteen feet of snow will get dumped on us. A fluffy bunny hops around, delivering baskets of chocolate eggs that kids can add to their Christmas and Valentine's candy stash.

Kidding! We're kidding! Of course, there's no such thing as "left over" candy! At least not at our houses. If you can make candy last from one holiday to another, you're a better parent than we are. (At least better at replenishing what you gobbled. When we bogart candy, we just tell the kids that that creepy Elf is still hanging around.)

If there's one season that parents can really get their brains around, it's spring. Indeed, parenting is the promise of spring fulfilled: We *spring* to catch a sudden spill before it hits the carpet. We *spring* to volunteer as room parents and chaperones. We (reluctantly) *spring* for the latest budget-busting gizmos and toys du jour. And, of course, we *spring* to tweet the day's side-splitting cuteness. After all that springing, it's finally time to sink into bed. Just one more chocolate egg. Last one. Swear!

My wife is getting rid of all the clutter. If you see the kids and me standing out by the street, it means we didn't make the cut this year.

— α geek (@AlfaGeeek)

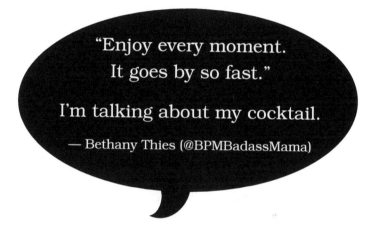

"Enjoy every moment. It goes by so fast."

I'm talking about my cocktail.

— Bethany Thies (@BPMBadassMama)

Me, prying a toy hammer from my 4yo:
"Stop. It's not hammer time!"
Parenting is lonely when nobody's there to hear your outdated references.

— Full Metal Mommy (@FullMetalMommy)

Can someone turn the wind off for my 3yo? He can't eat breakfast if it's windy out, which would make sense IF WE WERE EATING OUTSIDE.

— Jennifer Lizza (@OutsmartedMommy)

I'm at the age where the best thing about Friday night is not having to pack lunches for tomorrow.

— Hot Breakfast (@AmyDillon)

Sorry to disappoint, Son. But I'm gonna draw the line at holding hands while you poop.

— Deva Dalporto (@MyLifeSuckers)

4yo said he went potty, and I asked if it
was Number 1 or 2.
He said Number 7, and now
I'm terrified to go into the bathroom.

— La Vie En Meh (@TheAlexNevil)

If this car's a-rockin', I'm letting the kids kill each other in the backseat while the mister takes forever inside Home Depot.

— Amy Flory (@FunnyIsFamily)

4yo: Can I have Mountain Dew?
Me: No. Go to bed.
4yo: I'll need energy if zombies attack.
Me:
4yo:
Me: One can. Just in case.

— Exploding Unicorn (@XplodingUnicorn)

I try to explain to my kids during the movie that in reality, even a cowardly lion would definitely eat a girl and a little dog.

— Abe Yospe (@Cheeseboy22)

I don't have the heart to break it
to my little son that he won't become a
ninja by doing Tae Bo with his mom.

— Andy Herald (@AndyHerald)

A fun thing to do is sign your kids up for a class they're dying to take and then listen to them complain about it for the next eight weeks.

— Kate Hall (@KateWhineHall)

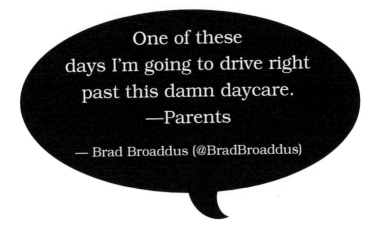

One of these days I'm going to drive right past this damn daycare.
—Parents

— Brad Broaddus (@BradBroaddus)

Me: Will you please put the pillows back on the couch?

4yo: No, it's a lot more relaxing when you do the work.

— Carisa Miller (@MCarisa)

My 3yo just corrected my math. When he gets out of time-out, he's my new accountant.

— Father With Twins (@FatherWithTwins)

Teen: That cake was literally to die for.
Me: I'm waiting.
Teen: Are you mocking me?
Me: I literally am.

— Linda Doty (@LindaInDisguise)

Me: Do you know about the boy who cried wolf?
5yo: Does he cry like a wolf?
Me: No, he—
5yo: Does he turn into a wolf?
Me: No! He—
5yo: Bor-ing!

— La Vie En Meh (@TheAlexNevil)

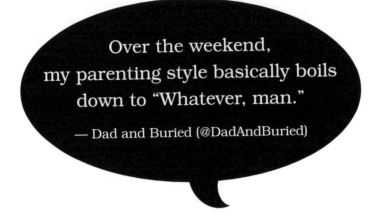

Over the weekend, my parenting style basically boils down to "Whatever, man."

— Dad and Buried (@DadAndBuried)

My husband is always asking me to send him dirty pictures. I should just give in and send him a picture of our bathroom.

— Bethany Thies (@BPMBadassMama)

My kids are perfectly reciting the list of Lucky Charms marshmallows, and I've never been more proud.

— Andy H. (@AndyAsAdjective)

I like to consider myself a positive person. I just tried to teach my kid how to tie his shoes, and I can't say I'm that person any longer.

— Jennifer Lizza (@OutsmartedMommy)

7yo: Can you sign this?

Me: Why?

7yo: My teacher says you have to.

Me: Can I read it?

7yo: No.

Me:

7yo: And sign with your eyes closed.

— Jen Good (@BuriedWithKids)

My 5yo is peeling her own hard-boiled egg because we have an hour to kill.

— Amy Flory (@FunnyIsFamily)

I just overheard one of my kids ask, "What do you think is grosser: Mom or creamed corn?"

So that's how my Mother's Day is going.

The Story Behind the Tweet:

Last Mother's Day, I overheard my kids giggling like crazy in the next room.

Awwww, listen to them, having so much fun together! I kvelled to myself.

But when the laughter morphed into squeals of "Ewwww!" and "GROSS!" I decided to investigate further. Fortunately, they were only playing "What's Grosser?" and not shaving their eyebrows ... again.

I hunkered by the door, reveling in their creativity.

When their comparisons graduated from basic bodily functions to more advanced scenarios like "kissing a dog's butt" and "plunging public toilets with your bare hand," I swelled with pride. My kids are funny!

And that's when it happened. My brilliant brood grew tired of poop, and compared ME, their mother, ON MOTHER'S DAY no less, to a canned starchy vegetable.

I was crestfallen. At least have the decency to pit me against something truly vile, like a vat of medical waste or the list of baby names rejected by Kimye.

Naturally, I handled it like any decent mother would—I gave them more material.

"Playtime's over. Whose turn is it to pluck Mama's neck hair?"

— Leslie Marinelli (@TheBeardedIris)

Took the 6yo into the ladies room.

6yo: Hey! That's not fair they sell napkins in your bathroom!

Me: You have no idea how unfair it truly is, Kiddo.

— Domestic Goddess (@DomesticGoddss)

14yo: If I ate at Carl's Jr. AND the chicken place, I'd get diabetes.

Dad: Well, it runs in the family.

14yo: Nobody runs in our family.

— Elleroy Was Here (@ModMomElleroy)

Me: We can't eat pizza for every meal.

4yo: The Ninja Turtles do and they're heroes.

I hate it when she beats me with science.

— Exploding Unicorn (@XplodingUnicorn)

15yo: I had leggings on this morning, but I decided I needed a pocket so I put on jeggings.
Me: I don't know what any of that means.

— KC of TX (@KCMoore51)

Fell asleep
on the couch at 7:45 p.m.,
proving I still got it.

And by "it" I mean
parenting-induced narcolepsy.

— Kim Bongiorno (@LetMeStart)

Take a shower at night: toddler wakes up.
Take a shower in the morning: toddler wakes up.
gets gym membership to take showers

— Lauren (@WorkingMom86)

My daughter wants to be a shrink when she grows up. Clearly I've failed to teach her our family's proper role in the psychiatric process.

— Housewife of Hell (@HousewifeOfHell)

Complaints with a side of whining and eye rolls. It's what's for dinner.

— Jennifer Lizza (@OutsmartedMommy)

We're trying to decide what to do for family vacation this summer. Personally, I'd like to go into my room and shut the door for a week.

— Steve Olivas (@SteveOlivas)

My son ordered grilled cheese for dinner then refused to eat it because "there is so much cheese. And bread."

— It's Really 10 Months (@Really10Months)

Of course I will guard your Easter basket from any pillaging by your sisters. Bring it here, Honey.

— Linda Doty (@LindaInDisguise)

Me: Do you know why I took your toy away?

5yo: You don't know?

— La Vie En Meh (@TheAlexNevil)

Hey a Slinky! This is cool, how do you do it again? It's tangled. Can we get another one?

The two-minute lifespan of every kid's Slinky.

— Simon Holland (@SimonCHolland)

When one door closes another one opens.

Unless it's me closing the bathroom door.
Then it's just my kids opening the same door.

— Jennifer Lizza (@OutsmartedMommy)

My kid just peed himself and then had a tantrum because he couldn't see his ear.

But congrats on your pregnancy!

— Marl's Beans (@MarleBean)

**2yo just pulled off a patch of my leg hair
with a sticker. It's like the world's
most depressing spa over here.**

— Bethany Thies (@BPMBadassMama)

For someone who
isn't allowed to sit down,
you'd think I'd be much skinnier.

— Jewel Nunez (@OneFunnyMummy)

This is your brain
holds up egg
This is your brain while raising kids
smears egg on every surface of house
grinds shell into your hair

— Lurk @ Home Mom (@LurkAtHomeMom)

Wish my kid would stop trying to help me do her school project so we can just get it finished.

— Simon Holland (@SimonCHolland)

My husband got a new car yesterday so I let the kids eat tortilla chips in it to remind him who's really in control here.

— Stella G. Maddox (@StellaGMaddox)

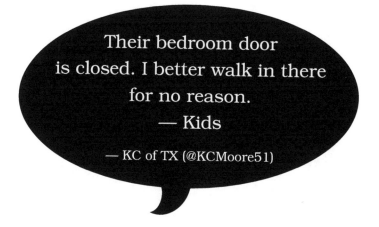

Their bedroom door
is closed. I better walk in there
for no reason.
— Kids

— KC of TX (@KCMoore51)

That stupid Tooth Fairy screwed up again and gave one of my kids more money than the other. Freaking home wrecker.

— Kate Hall (@KateWhineHall)

Mommy Milk Factory has officially closed down. Owner thanks her two loyal customers. Equipment will now be used for display purposes.

— Marl's Beans (@MarleBean)

Accidentally brought my daughter's fruity shower gel to the gym this morning, and now everyone is calling me grape nuts.

— Simon Holland (@SimonCHolland)

My kids just ate an entire bag of Hostess Donettes for breakfast. Unless you're with CPS, in which case they had oatmeal.

— QwertyGirl (@QwertyGirl)

My kids moved to another table at lunch when I called the waffle fries "hashtags."

— Housewife of Hell (@HousewifeOfHell)

The original scripture said, "It is easier for a camel to go through the eye of a needle than it is for a 7yo boy to do one hour of homework."

— Sarah del Rio (@Est1975Blog)

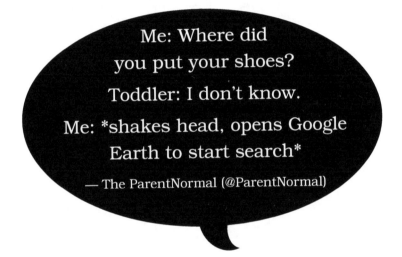

Me: Where did you put your shoes?

Toddler: I don't know.

Me: *shakes head, opens Google Earth to start search*

— The ParentNormal (@ParentNormal)

New mom: I'll call you right back. I have to pee.

Experienced mom: No commentary and no apology for the flush in the background.

— Stella G. Maddox (@StellaGMaddox)

If you're wondering whether it's possible to make a 3yo happy, mine just put his slippers in the trash because they were "too comfy."

— Lurk @ Home Mom (@LurkAtHomeMom)

Hubby took the kids downstairs and is letting me sleep in! I'm so excit—never mind. I hear crying already. I think it's my husband.

— Marl's Beans (@MarleBean)

Parenting,
when you eat the last
three cookies because you
have four children.

— Nicole Leigh Shaw (@NicoleLeighShaw)

I'm proud of my kids
but not "ruin my car with honor
roll bumper stickers" proud.

— Sarcastic Mommy (@SarcasticMommy4)

Not sure about other countries, but here "turn off the TV" roughly translates to "please explode like a screaming, flailing, spitting bomb."

— Andrea (@SheepAndRobots)

When my kids get into physical fights, I tell them to stop, breathe, and count to ten. This gives their dad and me time to bet on who'll win.

— Linda Doty (@LindaInDisguise)

> Never kick someone when they're down. Climb on their back and try to ride them like a horsie.
> — Kids

The Story Behind the Tweet:

"Share! I said SHARE!" I screeched. "Wait! NO! Don't share TOOTHBRUSHES! And don't forget to go potty!"

It was one of those days when I was racing against the clock, trying to get the kids ready for school and myself looking at least slightly presentable so we could leave the house. In the middle of this chaos, I was down on my hands and knees, cleaning up toys when suddenly, my 3yo climbed on my back, grabbed my hair and shouted, "Yeehaw, Sparky!"

I sat there for a moment. Maybe another day I would have gotten frustrated. The tweet flashed through my mind. I smirked, threw the toys in the basket, and galloped my son back into the bathroom. Neigh!

— Marl's Beans (@MarleBean)

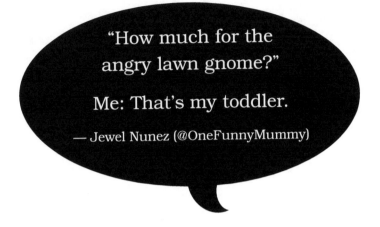

"How much for the angry lawn gnome?"

Me: That's my toddler.

— Jewel Nunez (@OneFunnyMummy)

90% of being a parent is shouting, "Remember to flush the toilet!" The other 10% is flushing the toilet for everyone.

— Paige Kellerman (@PaigeKellerman)

I wish my wife would stop telling the kids that Chewbacca is "kinda like a Bigfoot." They're two separate species from different galaxies.

— Pete Lynch (@PJTLynch)

"Watch the mother as she carefully
approaches the toddler with a pair of pants."
— What a *National Geographic* narrator
would say about my mornings.

— Lauren (@WorkingMom86)

Thinking about moving to Utah ... so we can get a couple more spouses in the mix to help get our 4yo to bed.

— Designer Daddy (@DesignerDaddy)

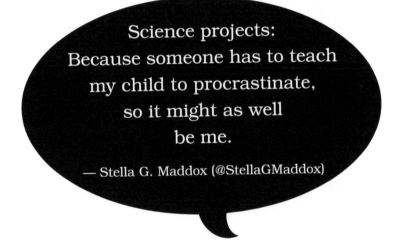

Science projects:
Because someone has to teach
my child to procrastinate,
so it might as well
be me.

— Stella G. Maddox (@StellaGMaddox)

They say the price of freedom is eternal vigilance. I say, it's $12–$20 per hour for a decent babysitter.

— Andrea (@SheepAndRobots)

I just spent four days organizing my son's Legos for him so that he could take out a mixing bowl, throw them all in it, and stir them with a spoon.

— Sarah del Rio (@Est1975Blog)

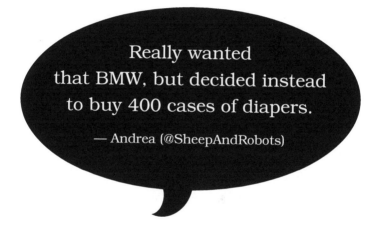

Really wanted
that BMW, but decided instead
to buy 400 cases of diapers.
— Andrea (@SheepAndRobots)

If anyone wants to come over, my kid's giving an epic recap of his Mario vs. Sonic Wii match. You can probably still make it for the second hour.

— Pete Lynch (@PJTLynch)

Hindsight. Those four minutes when the baby was sleeping and the older kids were playing Legos was my window to shower.

— It's Really 10 Months (@Really10Months)

8:00 p.m.
Me: G'night.
4yo: Will you check on me later?
Me: Yes.

8:01 p.m.
4yo: Why aren't you checking?
Me: I haven't left the room yet!

— The ParentNormal (@ParentNormal)

Want to find out if your OCD meds are working? Watch a kid open a new box of cereal.

— Simon Holland (@SimonCHolland)

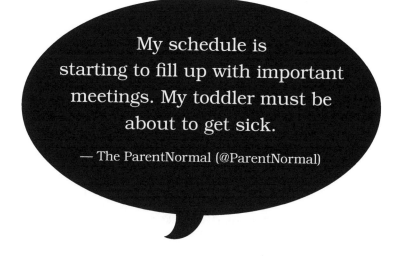

My schedule is starting to fill up with important meetings. My toddler must be about to get sick.

— The ParentNormal (@ParentNormal)

I like Twitter because having one-sided conversations with virtually no feedback reminds me a lot of being a parent.

— Steve Olivas (@SteveOlivas)

I'm glad I pay $200 a month for cable so my kids can leave the TV on as background noise while on their iPads.

— Sarcastic Mommy (@SarcasticMommy4)

Reasons your 4yo is pissed:

You didn't help him open his snack.

Oh, you did help him? NO! He can do it himself!!!

— Lurk @ Home Mom (@LurkAtHomeMom)

I would write a book of parenting tips but "Hide in bathroom with vodka" pretty much fits on a Post-It Note.

— Rodney Lacroix (@Moooooog35)

I'm never a more ineffective parent than when I accidentally make threats that rhyme.

— Paige Kellerman (@PaigeKellerman)

I love seeing a first-time dad at the circus when he realizes snow cones are $14. Welcome to the club, Buckaroo.

— Simon Holland (@SimonCHolland)

When a toddler misses a nap, it's like buying a lottery ticket. You may be lucky enough to go to bed early, but chances are, it just costs you.

— The ParentNormal (@ParentNormal)

No one can truly know the rage inside of a man until he is asked to put together a toddler's tricycle.

— La Vie En Meh (@TheAlexNevil)

I'm chaperoning a thirteen-hour middle school chorus field trip today ... because I have a flexible work schedule and I hate myself.

— Leslie Marinelli (@TheBeardedIris)

"It's Friday!"
I tell my toddler at breakfast.
As if that means anything
for either of us.

— Hot Breakfast (@AmyDillon)

On the one hand, my boy is learning Spanish and cool things about animals. On the other hand, I want to punch Diego in the face.

— Yuvi Zalkow (@YuviZalkow)

In a dinner discussion about what we would grow if we had a garden, my 4yo suggested "some balls."

— Amy Flory (@FunnyIsFamily)

> 3yo: Mommy, you need to know that if your head falls off, you do NOT get a new one.

The Story Behind the Tweet:

It's music to my ears when the boys share something fascinating they've learned about the world. Then, there are times they almost get it right, but ultimately miss the point completely. I've been told there ARE sewer lizards that WILL "travel up the pipes into the bathwater." They've caught me leaving the shower and agreed my "pee hole is sick" because "the winky fell off." And my older son recently confessed he knows about the "tiny babies living in the balls" between his legs. He's just waiting to hear when they will "hatch."

Other times, they retell obvious facts so earnestly you choke on your drink. The above tweet is about a distinction my 3yo made between worms and humans. He knew he could NOT survive losing his head like the playground worms. "I understand," I replied. "This is why you must ALWAYS wear your helmet." And it was too late; I'd tragically oversimplified.

That Sunday, he insisted on wearing his yellow duck-printed helmet to church, through the entire service and lunch that followed. My dad reminds me that the minute he convinced my son to part with the ridiculous headgear, he immediately stumbled and whacked his noggin.

— Andrea (@SheepAndRobots)

5yo: You're a good dad.

Me: What makes you say that?

5yo: Since all your grandmas and grandpas are dead, I thought I would give you a compliment.

— TchrQuotes (@TchrQuotes)

He peed in the toilet. I flushed it. He wants his pee back.

— Me, explaining to a friend on the phone why my 3yo is screaming hysterically

— Lurk @ Home Mom (@LurkAtHomeMom)

"Son, it's time we had the talk."

"About the birds and the bees?"

"No, about spiders. They're terrifying, and I'm sorry I screamed like your mother."

— Kalvin MacLeod (@KalvinMacLeod)

I just saved a bundle on future college tuition by finding out my 4yo wants to be a gumball when he grows up.

— Lurk @ Home Mom (@LurkAtHomeMom)

PART 2

Summer Breeze?

Ah, summer. Perhaps second only to Christmas in terms of eager anticipation and soul-sucking disappointment. A time when your precious Idea Of Summer, nurtured and coddled through the long, frigid winter, gets crushed like a sandcastle beneath your brood's teeny, tiny destructive feet even before you get your sunscreen on.

And with that, your visions of sunning by the pool, sipping cool drinks and reading any book not made of cardboard, are superseded:

C'mon! Let's move it! We gotta get to the pool before all the shady spots are taken!

Now, do I have snacks, sunscreen, floaties, drinks, goggles—

Yes! You have to wear shoes ... because the driveway will be hot ... just find them!

And dive toys, swim diapers, ice packs, lunches—

GET YOUR SUITS ON!

And sun hats, towels, change of clothes, beach chairs, pool passes, iced coffee? I'd better pack a carafe.

DID YOU HEAR ME?! LET'S GO!

You're exhausted and it's only 9 a.m. How many days till the kids go back to school?

Son: What animal kills people most? Bears?

Me: Mosquitos. Malaria is—

Son: MOM! MOSQUITOS CAN KILL ME!

And that's how I ruined summer already.

— Pete Lynch (@PJTLynch)

Hell hath no fury
like a 3yo who doesn't get to
push the elevator buttons.

— Dad and Buried (@DadAndBuried)

My husband brought home one Happy Meal for two kids. Frankly, things would have been less dramatic if he'd brought home a girlfriend.

— Full Metal Mommy (@FullMetalMommy)

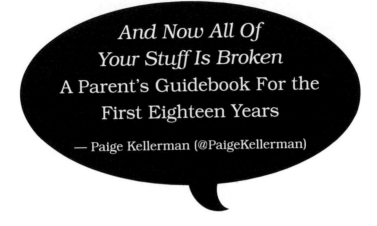

And Now All Of Your Stuff Is Broken
A Parent's Guidebook For the First Eighteen Years

— Paige Kellerman (@PaigeKellerman)

My daughter's counting cars as we drive down the road, like some kinda *Rain Man* nerd. She's up to 274, but she missed one about three miles back.

— Andy H. (@AndyAsAdjective)

15yo: I give up. The Wi-Fi always messes up when I try to FaceTime with my boyfriend.
Me: That's weird. *plugs router back in*

— KC of TX (@KCMoore51)

**Chips are not only delicious,
but if you crunch them loud enough
you can't hear your children anymore.**

— Jewel Nunez (@OneFunnyMummy)

I grounded my kid from electronics for a week and now he won't stop talking to me and I think I've made a horrible mistake.

— Stella G. Maddox (@StellaGMaddox)

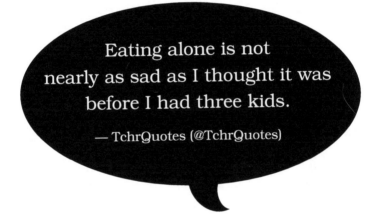

Eating alone is not nearly as sad as I thought it was before I had three kids.

— TchrQuotes (@TchrQuotes)

I asked the guy at the ticket counter if there's a reduced price for the movie if a mom plans on sleeping through most of it.

— QuestionableChoices (@QuestionableCIP)

Pulling the kids on an inner tube behind the boat.

Apparently that's not allowed on this particular highway.

— Brad Broaddus (@BradBroaddus)

How to get things done with kids in the house:
1. Set up a fun activity
2. Now quick, throw in some laundr—
3. Ok, they're bored, time's up

— Lurk @ Home Mom (@LurkAtHomeMom)

4yo: I put my Barbie in the tanning bed.
Me: You don't have a Barbie tanning bed.
4yo:
Me: *sprints to the toaster*

— Exploding Unicorn (@XplodingUnicorn)

By the time my 5yo is done with his dinner, it'll be time to start applying to colleges.

The Story Behind the Tweet:

One of my sons is the slowest eater in the world. I say this with complete confidence and without hyperbole. Four out of five days during the week, almost his entire lunch box will come back the way he took it to school because, according to his twin brother, "he just talks, and plays, and says silly things while everyone else eats."

The night I wrote this tweet, we started dinner at 5:30 p.m., and for once, I decided not to rush him. So, we just sat there, and he ate a bite every ten minutes while he sang songs, invented silly games for us to play, made funny faces, went to the bathroom twice, and finally finished his dinner at 7:30 p.m., which is his bedtime.

Actually, I'm lying. At 7:30, I threw away about a third of his food. I swear that child doesn't need food to survive—he just lives on impish charm.

— Father With Twins (@FatherWithTwins)

I'm not saying the toys had too much to drink at their tea party, but Elsa just went home with Darth Vader.

— Bethany Thies (@BPMBadassMama)

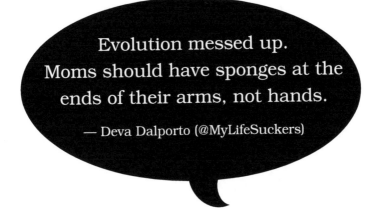

Evolution messed up.
Moms should have sponges at the ends of their arms, not hands.

— Deva Dalporto (@MyLifeSuckers)

Ant Rescue by 2yo:

1. Locate and smash.

2. Smear on book.

3. Shake book outside while repeating, "Go back to your home now, Ant."

— Carisa Miller (@MCarisa)

4yo: Mom, you look like a rock star in your glasses.

Me: Thanks!

4yo: No, I mean your sunglasses. In those glasses you look like Mr. Potato Head.

— Amy Flory (@FunnyIsFamily)

5yo: What's a cannibal?

Me: A person that eats another person.

5yo's eyes widen in horror.

Me: You said cannonball, didn't ya?

— Stephanie Jankowski (@CrazyExhaustion)

My 7yo son just told me the two-fingered peace sign means "Meet me in the shower at 2:00."

No more prison movies for that kid.

— Leslie Marinelli (@TheBeardedIris)

Superman saves toddler in street from speeding car

Superman: Next time make sure you're holding someone's h—

Toddler already in street

— The ParentNormal (@ParentNormal)

Churches get kind of mad when you drop your kids off in the nursery and then go to brunch.

— Simon Holland (@SimonCHolland)

"Did you seriously bring me to a party where there's no cake?"
— My 6yo's assessment of the neighborhood block party thus far

— Stella G. Maddox (@StellaGMaddox)

Funny how it's considered child abuse to shove your kid in a dark closet and close the door, but if you add a glow stick, it's fun.

— Zoe vs. the Universe (@ZoeVsUniverse)

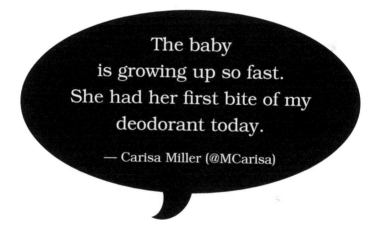

The baby
is growing up so fast.
She had her first bite of my
deodorant today.

— Carisa Miller (@MCarisa)

Oh, you're making an important phone call? Hold on, let me get my trumpet.
— Kids

— Lurk @ Home Mom (@LurkAtHomeMom)

gets awakened by tap on arm

"Daddy, can I buy a game on my Kindle?"

"What time is it?"

"5 a.m."

"I'm gonna close my eyes now and let you live, ok?"

— Andy H. (@AndyAsAdjective)

As a dad,
I definitely don't say
"Who's your daddy?"
as much as I thought I would.

— Creed (@NoviceFather)

There is a fine line between giving my children privacy in the bathroom and leaving them alone to eat toilet paper.

— Carisa Miller (@MCarisa)

It's terrifying watching your child get in the car and drive away for the first time. Especially when they're nine.

— Brad Broaddus (@BradBroaddus)

I had to pick up something I dropped behind my kids' toilet, so now I'm off to set my hand on fire.

— Kate Hall (@KateWhineHall)

So, if nobody saw me drop my son's waffle on the kitchen floor and then just stick it right back on his plate, it didn't happen, right?

— Sarah del Rio (@Est1975Blog)

"This ketchup is fantastic."

— My 5yo, after she insists on the most expensive entrée on the menu

— Stella G. Maddox (@StellaGMaddox)

My kids promised
no whining on my birthday,
so I guess their gift to me is
a pile of lies.

— Amy Flory (@FunnyIsFamily)

Me: Can I go play with my Twitter friends?
Wife: Are the kids in bed and the dishwasher emptied?
Me: ... Yes
wife opens cabinet, kids fall out

— Pete Lynch (@PJTLynch)

When the children ask, "Can we borrow the Cling Wrap?" it's usually time to investigate what's happening in the basement.

— Stella G. Maddox (@StellaGMaddox)

4yo: Can you do what you want at work?

Me: No, I have to listen to my boss.

4yo: Mom is at your work?

— Exploding Unicorn (@XplodingUnicorn)

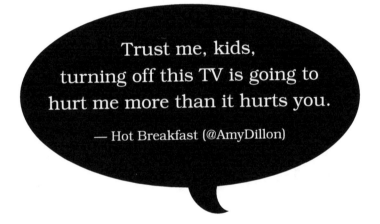

Trust me, kids,
turning off this TV is going to
hurt me more than it hurts you.

— Hot Breakfast (@AmyDillon)

Don't judge me by all the candy I eat. Judge me by all the candy I eat in front of my kids without getting caught. That's way more impressive.

— Wendy S. (@MaughamMom)

The 4yo saw picture of me pregnant. I explained that she was inside me. She thought for a bit then said, "I never want to do that again."

— Zoe vs. the Universe (@ZoeVsUniverse)

7yo just stomped out yelling, "Download me a new book!"

New tantrums for a new generation.

— α geek (@AlfaGeeek)

What did you have for dinner? I had second thoughts about having kids.

— Hot Breakfast (@AmyDillon)

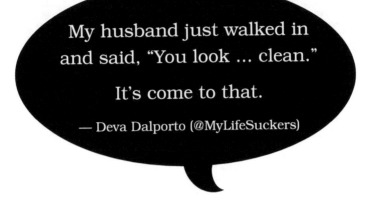

My husband just walked in and said, "You look ... clean."

It's come to that.

— Deva Dalporto (@MyLifeSuckers)

My bag is so full of my kids' crap that I'm starting to feel like Mary Poppins. If Mary Poppins can't find anything and swears a lot.

— Full Metal Mommy (@FullMetalMommy)

Me: How many chicken nuggets do you want tonight?
4yo: 100
Me: As a guide, you usually have four to six.
4yo (thinking): 30

— Zoe vs. the Universe (@ZoeVsUniverse)

Kid: If Mom was on *Wife Swap*, can you imagine how freaked out the other family would be?

The Story Behind the Tweet:

What can I say, I'm a frustrated actor/comedian. Since I never got my shot on Saturday Night Live, my husband and kids are forced to endure the constant pop culture references, celebrity impressions, and spontaneous song stylings that are part of the package when you live with me. My son, Max, once said to his Grandma, "See what we have to live with?" But after finishing a particularly satisfying rendition of Aerosmith's "Dream On," complete with full-on Steven Tyler moves and falsetto, the tweet above is what my older son said to my little guy as they both nodded knowingly.

— Elleroy Was Here (@ModMomElleroy)

If you do not stop arguing, I WILL turn this car around and around and around creating a time vortex, teleporting me back to before I had kids.

— McSweatervest (@McSwtrvst)

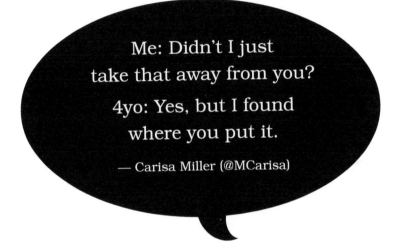

Me: Didn't I just
take that away from you?
4yo: Yes, but I found
where you put it.

— Carisa Miller (@MCarisa)

Just took my car in for service. They don't look under the seats, do they? It would be great if they didn't breathe in there either.

— Housewife of Hell (@HousewifeOfHell)

You never know just how much
you are willing to sacrifice as a mother
till you pull out your own ponytail holder
and give it to your child.

— Zoe vs. the Universe (@ZoeVsUniverse)

Right about now, the funk soul brothas are trying to convince their teenage children that they were once extremely popular.

— McSweatervest (@McSwtrvst)

It's when you and your spouse start referring to each other as "Mommy" and "Daddy" that you realize you're never having sex ever again.

— Dad and Buried (@DadAndBuried)

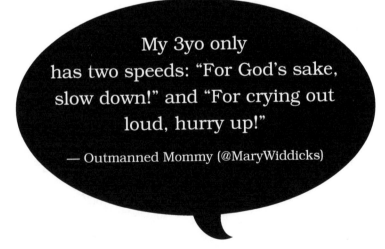

My 3yo only has two speeds: "For God's sake, slow down!" and "For crying out loud, hurry up!"

— Outmanned Mommy (@MaryWiddicks)

"Mom, will you drive me to Jane's? And stop on the way to get a gift for Katie? And drive my friends, too? And not talk at all the whole time?"

— Housewife of Hell (@HousewifeOfHell)

My kids just set up a lemonade stand. Older brother just charged younger brother for a cup. Capitalism.

— It's Really 10 Months (@Really10Months)

OMG!!!
I can't find my thing because it's put away in the place where it's supposed to go!
— Kids

— Jen Good (@BuriedWithKids)

What I say to my son: "Get dressed,"
His interpretation: "Stand around naked watching television with one sock on."

— Sarah del Rio (@Est1975Blog)

4yo: Mommy, you're just like a Disney movie. We should play pretend.
Me: Aww! Sure!
4yo: You can be the Beast.
Me: ...
4yo: Or the fat Sea Witch!

— Marl's Beans (@MarleBean)

What do I want for lunch? IDK. What's the thing you forgot to pick up at the store last night? I'll have that.
— 3yos

— Lurk @ Home Mom (@LurkAtHomeMom)

Based on the number of Band-Aid wrappers strewn about, one of my kids is bleeding out somewhere in this house.

— Linda Doty (@LindaInDisguise)

The moms who claim to love the book *Love You Forever* have clearly never woken up at 3 a.m. to find their mother-in-law cradling their husband.

— Pete Lynch (@PJTLynch)

3yo: *steps on scale* How much do I weigh?
Me: 34 lbs.
3yo: Oh, man. I can't wait till I weigh big numbers like you.
Me: *gets rid of scale*

— Jennifer Lizza (@OutsmartedMommy)

I'm watching a kids show about how everyone is special and has talents, and I want to see the episode where their mediocrity crushes them alive.

— McSweatervest (@McSwtrvst)

If you like eating, crapping, and showering at superhuman speeds all while enjoying none of it, then maybe parenting is for you.

— Creed (@NoviceFather)

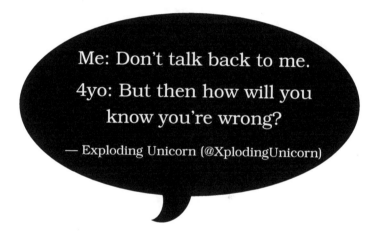

Me: Don't talk back to me.

4yo: But then how will you know you're wrong?

— Exploding Unicorn (@XplodingUnicorn)

My daughter woke up at 6:06 a.m. today instead of her usual 6:00 a.m. because we let her stay up five hours past her bedtime last night.

— Simon Holland (@SimonCHolland)

Waiting for my wife so I can get a break from the kids feels like waiting for the handoff in a relay race with the slowest teammate ever.

— Rodney Lacroix (@Moooooog35)

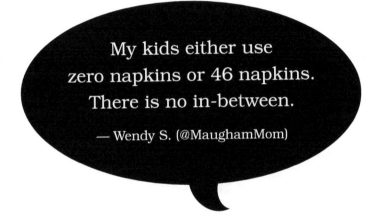

My kids either use
zero napkins or 46 napkins.
There is no in-between.

— Wendy S. (@MaughamMom)

My son just locked me out of the house, and I'm trapped on the shaded back deck. It's the nicest thing he's ever done for me.

— QuestionableChoices (@QuestionableCIP)

The trouble with establishing a rep with your kids that you are the dad who can fix anything, is spending four hours fixing a Happy Meal toy.

— a geek (@AlfaGeeek)

Since I've had kids,
all my fantasies involve silence.

— Stella G. Maddox (@StellaGMaddox)

My kid is almost old enough for social media so we'll need to have "the talk" soon. You know, about your/you're and their/there/they're.

— Linda Doty (@LindaInDisguise)

This is how my husband "puts our son to bed":

*tells son "it's time for bed"
*does nothing else

— Sarah del Rio (@Est1975Blog)

"Oh really? 'Cuz my son gave me this, and I find it difficult to believe there are TWO #1 Dad coffee mugs, so yours is obviously a knock off."

— La Vie En Meh (@TheAlexNevil)

Which takes longer, a twenty-minute walk with your 4yo in a stroller or a five-minute walk with a 4yo on foot?

Answer: shoot me.

— Zoe vs. the Universe (@ZoeVsUniverse)

What I say: I'm taking a nap.

What they hear: Got a problem? Need something? Just want to talk? I'm here for you, and now's the perfect time.

— QwertyGirl (@QwertyGirl)

My toddler just grabbed a slice of pizza, folded it like a pro and took a bite. It was like watching a paternity test come back positive.

— Simon Holland (@SimonCHolland)

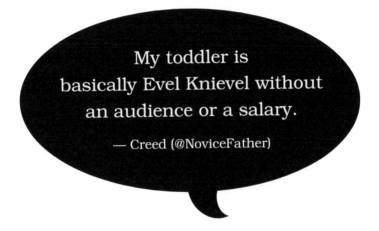

My toddler is basically Evel Knievel without an audience or a salary.

— Creed (@NoviceFather)

I'm glad my son was around to warn me that my dinner was hot and helped me out by blowing and spitting on it.

— Lauren (@WorkingMom86)

Returned home from a three-day conference to my kids singing "Cat's in the Cradle."

I should probably start saving for elder care.

— Leslie Marinelli (@TheBeardedIris)

My 18mo is trying to sweep the carpet with a broom.

THE CARPET. Babies don't know how to clean ANYTHING.

— TchrQuotes (@TchrQuotes)

Me: Want a banana?
3yo: Yes, but don't cut it up. And don't peel it. And don't make it be a banana. Make it be a waffle.

— Wendy S. (@MaughamMom)

My kids just offered to change bedtime to 5:30 if I pay them a one-time fee of a million dollars, so I'm here asking you to give what you can.

— Kalvin MacLeod (@KalvinMacLeod)

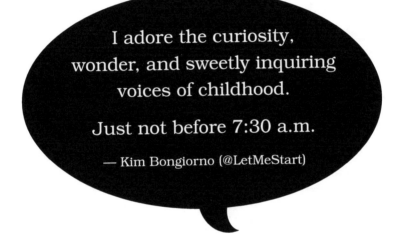

I adore the curiosity, wonder, and sweetly inquiring voices of childhood.

Just not before 7:30 a.m.

— Kim Bongiorno (@LetMeStart)

My wife texted me and said she's on her way home with our son, and the only thing I'm hoping for now is traffic.

— Creed (@NoviceFather)

You bring a baby monitor to the bar one time, and everyone freaks out.

— Simon Holland (@SimonCHolland)

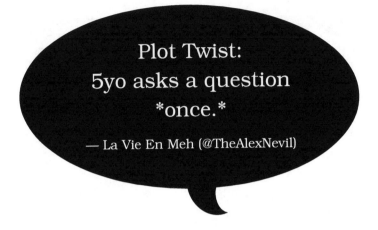

Plot Twist:
5yo asks a question
once.

— La Vie En Meh (@TheAlexNevil)

The cat is crying because she wants to get away from the kids. Sorry, cat. From experience I can tell you that it doesn't work.

— Stella G. Maddox (@StellaGMaddox)

Clean Toddler and Eating Toddler are like Clark Kent and Superman. You never see them at the same time.

— The ParentNormal (@ParentNormal)

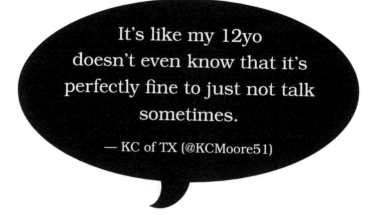

It's like my 12yo doesn't even know that it's perfectly fine to just not talk sometimes.

— KC of TX (@KCMoore51)

Me: This is your weekend with the kids. Mine is next weekend.

Him: But we're not divorced.

Me: Don't ruin my fantasy!

— Linda Doty (@LindaInDisguise)

By the noise my kids are making, they're either destroying the downstairs or building an addition. I hope it's a bonus room with a bar.

— Jennifer Lizza (@OutsmartedMommy)

"Will I ever live in a clean house again?"

Shakes Magic 8 ball

Magic 8 ball explodes and makes a mess

The Story Behind the Tweet:

I was cleaning up after dinner, and my son was spreading his toys all over the living room. "Whatever," I thought. "I'll clean that up after he goes to bed." As I was finishing the dishes, my son ran in because he needed to use the potty. We ran to the bathroom where, in all the excitement, he peed all over the wall.

That night, I learned that the amount of time it takes me to clean a pee-splattered bathroom is the same amount of time my son needs to create a new Crayola masterpiece on the living room wall.

"Will I ever live in a clean house again?" I wondered as I assessed the damage to the living room. After I picked up the toys and scrubbed down the wall, I grabbed the glass of wine I'd poured two hours earlier. I sat down, took a sip, and found a Hot Wheels car in my glass.

— Lauren (@WorkingMom86)

If you run down the hallway of a hotel shouting "I'M A SECRET NINJA!!" you're doing it wrong.

— Designer Daddy (@DesignerDaddy)

My "mom voice" was so loud even the neighbors washed their hands and cleaned their rooms.

— Wendy S. (@MaughamMom)

Do you
mind if my extremely
obnoxious friend comes over
and eats all our food?
— Kids

— KC of TX (@KCMoore51)

Ways teens communicate with Mom:

Eye roll

K text

"OMG NO"

Silence

Sigh

Humming to self

Rapid text clicking

Yelling

— Housewife of Hell (@HousewifeOfHell)

"This is a funny necklace!"
—3yo with my thong around her neck

— Amy Flory (@FunnyIsFamily)

PART 3
Free Fall

With autumn come crisp mornings, the crunch of fallen leaves, pumpkin-spiced everything and tax-free shopping days, which can only mean one thing: THE KIDS ARE GOING BACK TO SCHOOL! WOOT WOOT! Let's get ready to reeee-laaaaax! Finally! After a summer of sunburned noses, sandy towels and screeching shrieks about whose turn it is to choose a DVD and endless rounds of I Know You Are, But What Am I? you can finally have a little peace and quiet.

Oh, honey. You've earned it. It's just, well, don't

get too comfortable. Because as soon as the kids get home there's homework. And soccer practice. And 7 a.m. games on Saturdays. And piano lessons. And scouts. And more homework. And STEM class. And PTO. And homework. And the All Whiners Chorus doing their renditions of *My teacher hates me!* and *But Olivia's mom got HER an iPhone (Sulk Sulk, Pout Pout)*. Oh, and did we mention, homework?

But don't worry. You'll make it. Only ten more months till summer!

I'm just a guy standing in front of a girl begging her to remember where she put her other shoe because we are late for preschool.

— Simon Holland (@SimonCHolland)

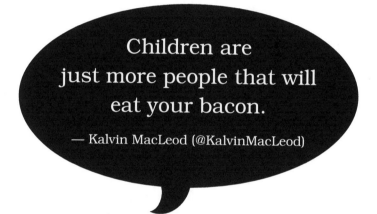

Children are just more people that will eat your bacon.

— Kalvin MacLeod (@KalvinMacLeod)

I have mixed feelings, but I mostly admire the 2yo's ability to show up completely naked to dinner and still demand hot Spaghettios.

— Paige Kellerman (@PaigeKellerman)

Oh, we're leaving now? Ok, gimme one sec, I just need to take off my shoes and throw a tantrum about cupcakes. Then we can go.
— My 2yo

— Lurk @ Home Mom (@LurkAtHomeMom)

There's half a bagel on the counter ... I think only one kid licked it. It's yours if you want it.
— How I make breakfast for my husband

— Jen Good (@BuriedWithKids)

Imagine the nastiest possible thing you could find on the floor right now.

Wrong.

It's already in my toddler's mouth.

— Hot Breakfast (@AmyDillon)

"You're not the boss of me,"
I whisper under my breath, as I make
four different lunches for my kids.

— Sarcastic Mommy (@SarcasticMommy4)

My daughter put a horse's head in my bed this morning. It was from an animal cracker, but it pretty clearly conveyed who's boss.

— Simon Holland (@SimonCHolland)

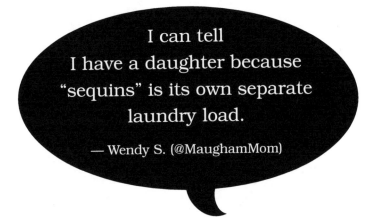

I can tell
I have a daughter because
"sequins" is its own separate
laundry load.

— Wendy S. (@MaughamMom)

Three kids have mistaken me for their mom today which tells me my greasy ponytail and under-eye bags are on-trend.

— Amy Flory (@FunnyIsFamily)

"Are there any hookers there?"
— 3yo wondering about a place to hang her coat at gymnastics

— Amy Flory (@FunnyIsFamily)

I graduated with honors from a highly esteemed college, and now I have to bribe my 5yo with candy to get him to put on pants.

— Father With Twins (@FatherWithTwins)

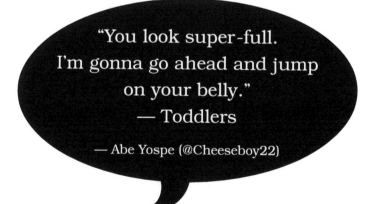

"You look super-full.
I'm gonna go ahead and jump
on your belly."
— Toddlers

— Abe Yospe (@Cheeseboy22)

My 4yo's preschool sent home a baking assignment for "homework." How fun! I'm thanking them by feeding him Pixie Sticks for breakfast today.

The Story Behind the Tweet:

The day had finally arrived, my little baby had started preschool! He'd sung songs, finger-painted and played with other kids. And the best part? Someone else had been in charge of the whole thing!

A dream come tru—wait. What was that in his backpack? It couldn't be. He was only four years old! NO. It couldn't be starting already ...

"Sweetie, it looks like you have homewor—Hey! Where did you go?" He'd disappeared into his room for some well-earned playtime.

Okay. It had to be something easy that he could do independently, right? Maybe he'd have to draw a picture or collect sticks or—nope. It was a cooking assignment! Of course! Because four-year-olds are notoriously great in the kitchen. So fun and totally not messy at all!

And with that, I had my first homework assignment in more than ten years.

"Make a dish that represents your heritage." Fan-flippin-tastic. Surely my mother had at least ONE of my Italian grandma's recipes that hadn't been pulled straight out of the Betty Crocker Cookbook.

"Hello, Mom? Help me, please!"

And with that, my mother had HER first homework assignment in more than thirty-five years.

— Lurk @ Home Mom (@LurkAtHomeMom)

If Spider-Man took as long to put on his costume as my son takes to put on his Spidey PJs, we'd all be dead now.

— Designer Daddy (@DesignerDaddy)

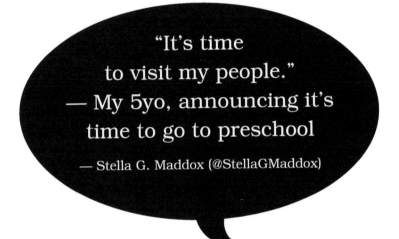

"It's time to visit my people."
— My 5yo, announcing it's time to go to preschool

— Stella G. Maddox (@StellaGMaddox)

My husband's tombstone is going to say: "Husband and father of four." Because it's impressive and also a detailed description of what killed him.

— Bethany Thies (@BPMBadassMama)

Boy tattling on his sister: "MOMMY! she poked my eyeballs out!"
Me: If I go down there and his eyes are still in his head, I'm gonna be pissed.

— QuestionableChoices (@QuestionableCIP)

The baby gets furious when I try to undress him.

He gets that from his mother.

— Brad Broaddus (@BradBroaddus)

Me: Remember how you'd pretend you didn't hear the kids cry?
Him: Yeah?
Me: That's what I do when they need help with algebra homework.

— Linda Doty (@LindaInDisguise)

"Daddy, can I go to work with you?"

"Aww Sweetie, I'd take you but you have school."

"Today's a school holiday."

"Aww Sweetie, I was lying then."

— Andy H. (@AndyAsAdjective)

3yo: I want a corn dog for dinner!

Me: *orders it*

10 min later

3yo: Dad, what's a corn dog?

Me: *realizes my dinner is now a corn dog*

— Father With Twins (@FatherWithTwins)

4yo: Why can we see through glass?

Me: I can't. You must have x-ray vision.

4yo:

Me: Tell no one.

— Exploding Unicorn (@XplodingUnicorn)

2yo held out her finger so I kissed it, expecting a boo-boo.
"Mom, why did you kiss my booger?"
Lesson learned.

— Wendy S. (@MaughamMom)

5yo: Mommy, go get my milk cup.

Wife: You're old enough to get it yourself.

5yo: I'M NOT YOUR SLAVE.

Wait. What?

The Story Behind the Tweet:

When I heard the harsh order to his mom for his beverage of choice, I thought, "Uh oh! Cranky McDemanderson is headed for trouble." I figured things might go smoothly once I heard her calm reply, but NOPE! He brought out a back-talk flamethrower he didn't even know how to use with his slave response. We had no idea where he picked it up, and we were both so shocked, we just laughed. He was not happy about our response. At all.

— Andy Herald (@AndyHerald)

People who say they don't have a favorite child have never had one feed them M&Ms while the other gets cracker crumbs all over the couch.

— Amy Flory (@FunnyIsFamily)

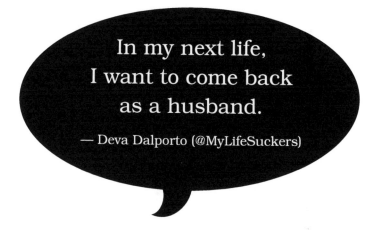

In my next life,
I want to come back
as a husband.

— Deva Dalporto (@MyLifeSuckers)

Thank God for texting, so my kids don't have to wait until they get home from school to lay their one-star lunch reviews on me.

— Elleroy Was Here (@ModMomElleroy)

Tonight's bedtime conversation topics with the 9yo included math, staplers, Minecraft, and how I sent him to his room once in December, 2013.

— Kim Bongiorno (@LetMeStart)

Oh, you think just because I'm married with kids that I no longer have game?

jumps in minivan, squeals out of library

— Brad Broaddus (@BradBroaddus)

Showering with an infant is how I imagine it would be to shower with a freshly basted Butterball turkey.

A screaming Butterball turkey.

— Creed (@NoviceFather)

Accidentally played dad instead of dead when I encountered a bear, and now it can ride a bike without training wheels.

— Simon Holland (@SimonCHolland)

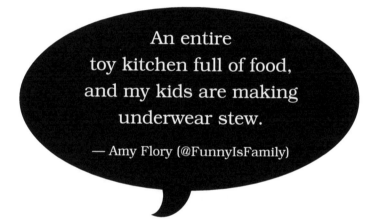

An entire
toy kitchen full of food,
and my kids are making
underwear stew.

— Amy Flory (@FunnyIsFamily)

"I like meat, pasta, and cheese ... unless you mix them all together ... then I don't."
— 7yo, contemplating lasagna

— Domestic Goddess (@DomesticGoddss)

"Mama, do you know what the easiest thing to make out of rock is? A ROCK."

Proof the line between great philosophy and 7yo crazy talk is slim.

— Kim Bongiorno (@LetMeStart)

My 6yo son to my 3yo daughter: "You keep erupting. Your mouth is a word volcano."

He gets it already, guys. He gets it.

— Wendy S. (@MaughamMom)

At meal time, I find it's most convenient to keep my glass of milk a nanometer from the edge of the table, next to my swinging elbow.
— Kids

— Kate Hall (@KateWhineHall)

I admire your optimism, busboy
sweeping under my son only
halfway through lunch.

— Marl's Beans (@MarleBean)

When my kids grow up, I'm going to knock on their doors at night and demand to know what's for dinner. Then I'll cry and use all the ketchup.

— Jennifer Lizza (@OutsmartedMommy)

Text to babysitter: "Whatever you do, don't get them wet or let them eat after midnight."

— MommaUnfiltered (@MommaUnfiltered)

My son's math skills are at their finest whenever he's calculating how late he can hand in his homework without failing.

— Housewife of Hell (@HousewifeOfHell)

I enjoy watching sports with my kids so I can answer questions like What color is the blue team? and What happens when a bear loses its arm?

— Kalvin MacLeod (@KalvinMacLeod)

Dance like nobody is watching.

Really speeds up the checkout process when back-to-school shopping with your teens.

— Leslie Marinelli (@TheBeardedIris)

How to RSVP to a kid party:
1. Pretend you have better things to do
2. Realize you don't have better things to do
3. RSVP "Can't wait!"
4. Cry

— Lurk @ Home Mom (@LurkAtHomeMom)

7yo: You're going to forget.

Me: No, I won't. Why would I forget?

7yo: Because old women forget stuff.

— Sarah del Rio (@Est1975Blog)

[in church]

4yo: *makes lightsaber noises*

Wife: Stop.

Me: I'll handle this.

takes kid to the cry room

has a lightsaber duel

— Exploding Unicorn (@XplodingUnicorn)

That's disgusting! Where did you learn to do that?! Don't wipe boogers on Mommy's pillow!

Wipe them on Daddy's.

— Marl's Beans (@MarleBean)

I wish I loved anything as much as my kids love getting out EVERY TOY THEY OWN five minutes before bedtime.

— Father With Twins (@FatherWithTwins)

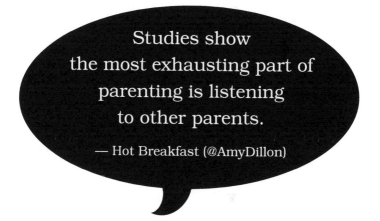

Studies show
the most exhausting part of
parenting is listening
to other parents.

— Hot Breakfast (@AmyDillon)

Out to lunch with my kids today and the server asks, "Anything I can take away from the table?"

"How about 4 kids?"

— Sarcastic Mommy (@SarcasticMommy4)

"If you clean it, they will come ... and destroy it ... immediately."
— *Field of Dreams 2, Housecleaning with Kids*

— Marl's Beans (@MarleBean)

4yo: Daddy, you can have this Parmesan bread bite.
Me: Aww, thank you, Sweetie. *eats bread bite*
4yo: I licked the Parmesan off for you.

— Andy H. (@AndyAsAdjective)

Fatherhood diary:
Day 1: They are beautiful
Day 8: They are noisy
Day 245: They are fun
Day 723: They are assholes
Day 1088: They are me

— Kalvin MacLeod (@KalvinMacLeod)

"Very colorful, fun. I'd put it in my mouth."
"A bit scary, seems sharp. Still, I'd
put it in my mouth."
— Baby reviews of stuff on the floor

— Pete Lynch (@PJTLynch)

Me: Eat your veggies. They'll make you big and strong like Chuck Norris. You wanna be like Chuck, right?

6yo: Don't oversell it, Mom.

— Elleroy Was Here (@ModMomElleroy)

Dear kids,

The 1st time was funny.

The 2nd time was a recap.

The 3rd was mildly agitating.

...

The 493rd time is shut the hell up.

— Stella G. Maddox (@StellaGMaddox)

Being a parent is a constant battle between going to bed to catch up on some sleep or staying awake to finally get a little alone time.

— Dad and Buried (@DadAndBuried)

I had been planning all day to talk to my kids about responsibility, but I forgot to pick them up from school.

— Brad Broaddus (@BradBroaddus)

"Mom, if you die right now, I'll use your phone and have Dad pick me up." Feeling the love.

— Leslie Marinelli (@TheBeardedIris)

15yo: I cleaned my ears and blood came out.
Me: Well, don't tell your mom unless you wanna spend your whole Sunday in the ER.

— KC of TX (@KCMoore51)

4yo promised if I left the overnight diaper off she would not pee in her bed. I was wrong to doubt her. She peed in mine.

— Zoe vs. the Universe (@ZoeVsUniverse)

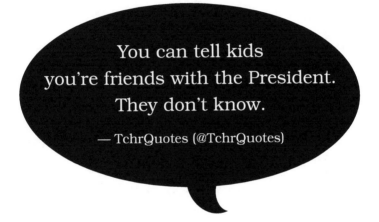

You can tell kids
you're friends with the President.
They don't know.

— TchrQuotes (@TchrQuotes)

Daughter: [5:45 a.m.] Daddy, can you make me breakfast?
Me: Can you not reach your Halloween candy?

— Simon Holland (@SimonCHolland)

I just napped, while sitting up, with my kids playing around me. I should be ashamed, but I'm too impressed with myself for shame.

— QuestionableChoices (@QuestionableCIP)

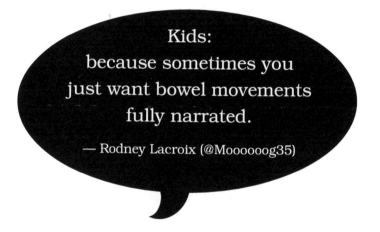

Kids:
because sometimes you
just want bowel movements
fully narrated.

— Rodney Lacroix (@Moooooog35)

At the store:
Me: We need to put all the toys back now, so people can buy them.
2yo: I'm people.

— Carisa Miller (@MCarisa)

My daughter just made a birthday card for my husband that says, "I will never forget you."

Does she know something I don't know?

— Deva Dalporto (@MyLifeSuckers)

Me: Son, sometimes you have to learn from your mistakes.
4yo: Daddy, I gave you that candy to hold for me.
Me: Yes, and that was a mistake.

— La Vie En Meh (@TheAlexNevil)

Me: You should ask for something else.
6yo: Why?
Me: What if Santa is all out of iPod Touches?
6yo: *disgusted* Did you forget he's MAGICAL?

— TchrQuotes (@TchrQuotes)

My 4yo cheated and beat me at Tic-Tac-Toe.
Trying to figure out how best to handle this.
So far I've just torn up the paper
and started crying.

— Andy H. (@AndyAsAdjective)

JUST GET IN THE FREAKIN' CAR SO WE CAN HAVE A FUN DAY AS A FAMILY AT THE FRICKIN' FARM!!!

— Kim Bongiorno (@LetMeStart)

Just finished crunching the numbers and it looks like my 19yo owes me about $1.8M.

— MommaUnfiltered (@MommaUnfiltered)

My kids watch Food Network then beg me to let them cook. Why can't someone start Laundry Network or Vacuuming Network?

— QwertyGirl (@QwertyGirl)

Me: Peyton Manning is looking old.

7yo: That's something you have in common with him!

Me:

— Sarah del Rio (@Est1975Blog)

Thanksgiving: a meal where parents make eight different dishes their kids won't eat instead of the usual three.

— Linda Doty (@LindaInDisguise)

"Dad, why's it called Black Friday?"

"Dunno."

"I thought you knew everything."

sees respect drain from her eyes

"THEY PAINT THE STORES BLACK."

"Cool."

— Andy H. (@AndyAsAdjective)

Parenting is the most beautiful and easy thing in the world when I'm drinking at a bar and talking to strangers about parenting.

The Story Behind the Tweet:

One evening at a neighborhood bar, I met this young couple who had just moved to our city. The woman was an aspiring writer, and when she complained about her struggle to write after working her day job, I shared some of my tricks for fitting writing into my busy life. When they heard that in addition to my writing life, I had a day job and a family, they were impressed. I'd had several gin and tonics, and I went on and on about how wonderful parenting was.

I was feeling pretty full of myself by the time I got

home ... where I found that the house was a mess and my son was up way past his bedtime, perched on top of his dresser, sobbing. My head started aching. Meanwhile, my son was inconsolable. Apparently, as I gradually learned, he was upset because he regretted the birthday gift he asked for and received SIX MONTHS AGO. Parenting is a lot easier from the bar.

— Yuvi Zalkow (@YuviZalkow)

I learned a lot during tonight's Family Nerf Gun War. For example, I WILL sacrifice my daughter for a clear shot at my husband.

— Wendy S. (@MaughamMom)

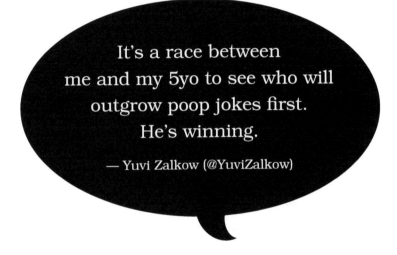

It's a race between me and my 5yo to see who will outgrow poop jokes first. He's winning.

— Yuvi Zalkow (@YuviZalkow)

My 5yo wears a tiara to preschool every day. She's the perfect example of dressing for the job you want.

— Stella G. Maddox (@StellaGMaddox)

In my defense, nobody told me
that my son's high-school orientation,
which was called "Wolverine Day,"
wasn't an X-Men cosplay event.

— Leslie Marinelli (@TheBeardedIris)

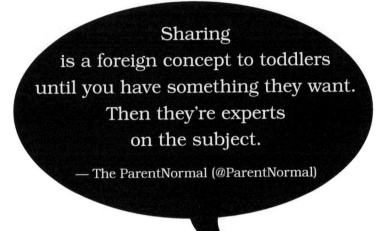

Sharing
is a foreign concept to toddlers
until you have something they want.
Then they're experts
on the subject.

— The ParentNormal (@ParentNormal)

Hey teachers, stop giving my kids homework that includes crap for me to do. I HAVE ALREADY GRADUATED.

Sincerely,
Every Parent Everywhere

— Rodney Lacroix (@Moooooog35)

**17yo daughter: I feel as if I've lost you
to the Twitterverse, Father.
Me: What?!? No! ...
17yo: You're going to tweet that, aren't you?**

— Steve Olivas (@SteveOlivas)

PART 4
Winter Bites

Shakespeare wrote that "Winter tames man, woman and beast." And you'll notice he very pointedly left children completely out of it. The bard knew. You might tame a shrew, but there's no taming *them*. Especially when you've been trapped inside for weeks on end by arctic temps or rampant illness. We get it. Locked in with toddlers and preschoolers, even the coziest home starts to feel like an upholstered prison (no matter how large your Netflix queue is).

But ohhhh, winter's dueling personalities can give a parent some wicked whiplash. There's the joy and merriment of the holiday season smacked back by the storm and stress of school breaks, snow days, phlegmy coughs and drippy noses. There are THE PARTIES! The prep work. THE GIFTS! The bills. THE GOODIES! The calories. THE EXPECTATIONS! The disappointments. THE FAMILY GET-TOGTHERS! The family get-togethers. It's no wonder parents beg Santa for one-way tickets to Cozumel. Who's in?

If you're wondering how many times you can refer to "Skylanders" as "Zoolander" before your 5yo gets pissed off, it's two.

— Designer Daddy (@DesignerDaddy)

At grocery store with in-laws
Mother-in-law: Is this your cart?
Me: The one with my children in it?
Mother-in-law: Yeah.
Me: ... Yes. That's my cart.

— Marl's Beans (@MarleBean)

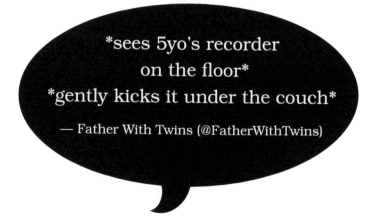

*sees 5yo's recorder
on the floor*
gently kicks it under the couch
— Father With Twins (@FatherWithTwins)

Nothing reveals a rookie more than a kindergarten parent who stays for the whole elementary school winter concert.

— QwertyGirl (@QwertyGirl)

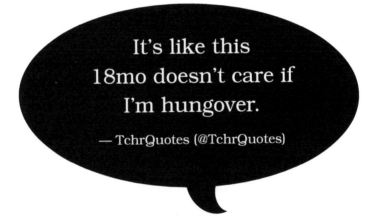

It's like this 18mo doesn't care if I'm hungover.

— TchrQuotes (@TchrQuotes)

Pretty disappointed to find out that "Toys for Tots" isn't a program where I trade my kids' toys for delicious tater tots.

— Abe Yospe (@Cheeseboy22)

5yo: My stomach hurts.

Me: Does it hurt a lot or a little?

5yo: It's kinda—

5yo vomits a lot

5yo: It's kinda—

Me: That's ok. I think I can guess.

— La Vie En Meh (@TheAlexNevil)

The saddest thing I have ever seen is my son trying to carve a Playstation 3 out of a giant lump of coal on Christmas.

— Abe Yospe (@Cheeseboy22)

17yo daughter: Can we turn down gramma's thermostat?

Me: It might kill your grandfather.

17yo: It'll cremate him at this temperature.

— Steve Olivas (@SteveOlivas)

On school-closing days, I like to start my morning off with a hot mug of my own salty tears.

— Nicole Leigh Shaw (@NicoleLeighShaw)

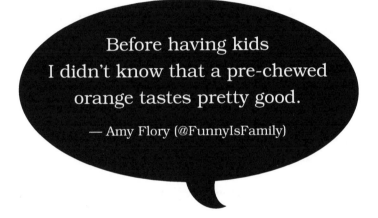

Before having kids
I didn't know that a pre-chewed
orange tastes pretty good.
— Amy Flory (@FunnyIsFamily)

My kids have built me the best retirement community I could ever hope for. I'll just need to figure out how to live in Minecraft.

— Linda Doty (@LindaInDisguise)

**You don't know fear until
a small child unexpectedly
zips a jacket up to your chin fat.**

— Paige Kellerman (@PaigeKellerman)

Me: Hello?

School Nurse: Sir, your 11yo is here with me, and he's complaining of a "crick in his neck."

Me: Just go ahead and put him down.

— KC of TX (@KCMoore51)

That $100 Lego set just paid for itself with the nap I was able to take.

— Hot Breakfast (@AmyDillon)

It gets awkward when we're in line at the grocery store and my 4yo son says, "So how many penises are in our family?"

— Yuvi Zalkow (@YuviZalkow)

4yo: Why are you always on Twitter?

Me: I'm talking to my friends.

4yo: It's ok. I have imaginary friends too.

— Exploding Unicorn (@XplodingUnicorn)

My sons have started calling me "Dad" instead of "Daddy"

lower lip quiver

I'm going to feed them nothing but baby food until they switch back.

— Father With Twins (@FatherWithTwins)

Every laundry basket in this house is overflowing. Probably time to buy more laundry baskets.

— QuestionableChoices (@QuestionableCIP)

4yo: When I'm big, I'll be a taxi driver.

Me: Well, by then robots will drive cars.

Now he's sad and hates robots, and that's why I'm a crappy dad.

The Story Behind the Tweet:

Ever since my son was little, whenever you would ask him what he wanted to be when he grew up, he'd say, "a taxi driver." We have no idea why. We live in a suburban area. I don't think the kid's ever been in a taxi. But he has his heart set on it.

One day when he was about four, he mentioned it again. I'd recently read an article about Google's self-driving cars, and not being one to think before speaking, I said, "By the time you're old enough to drive a car, they'll all be driven by robots!"

He turned to me, eyes filling with tears. In the pained, shocked voice of a kid who just found out his mom's been eaten by a shark, he shouted "No! No, Daddy! Robots will not drive cars! I hate robots!" He continued to freak out while I sat there feeling like an idiot.

A little while later, he added that he wanted to be "a singer on the radio," but also drive a taxi. My wife laughed, "Well, that's nice! You'll be able to listen to yourself sing while you drive your taxi." He seemed quite pleased with that.

— Pete Lynch (@PJTLynch)

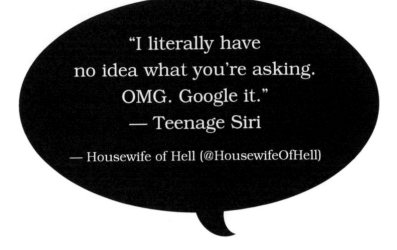

"I literally have
no idea what you're asking.
OMG. Google it."
— Teenage Siri

— Housewife of Hell (@HousewifeOfHell)

My daughter just told me she's moving out at fifteen. Then my son said he's never moving out. Not sure which terrifies me more.

— Deva Dalporto (@MyLifeSuckers)

Hey kids, do you guys want leftovers you won't eat or a new meal lovingly prepared that you won't eat?

— Bethany Thies (@BPMBadassMama)

I've looked everywhere in this minivan and can't seem to find my will to live.

— Brad Broaddus (@BradBroaddus)

Parenting rule #472: The parent who makes a kid laugh so hard he pukes is the one cleaning the car seat.

— Amy Flory (@FunnyIsFamily)

at work

"I try not to bring my home life into work."

drops purse

Hot Wheels and animal crackers fall everywhere

— Lauren (@WorkingMom86)

Just the other day, I asked my mom at what age children start really listening to their parents, but I don't remember what her answer was.

— Andy H. (@AndyAsAdjective)

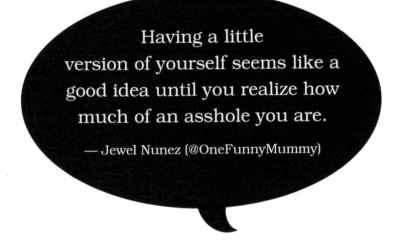

Having a little version of yourself seems like a good idea until you realize how much of an asshole you are.

— Jewel Nunez (@OneFunnyMummy)

Left the house with a potty-training 3yo and no backup clothes, so I know a little something about living on the edge.

— Wendy S. (@MaughamMom)

My 2yo just shouted, "What the hell?!?"

I'd be mad, but she said it when we ran out of Cheez-Its, so it seemed appropriate.

— Exploding Unicorn (@XplodingUnicorn)

I love the "work at home" option on snow days. The 6yo plays the boss, the 7yo portrays the annoying guy in the next cubicle, and the 14yo is the lazy intern.

— Domestic Goddess (@DomesticGoddss)

It's so cold today, I just grabbed the first two kids that got off the bus.

They look like nice kids; the redhead seems a little feisty.

— MommaUnfiltered (@MommaUnfiltered)

A cute thing I tell my kids when we see a dead deer on the side of the road is, "Looks like Santa lost his temper again."

— Abe Yospe (@Cheeseboy22)

12yo: We got a new kid in our class.
Me: Cool.
12yo: I can already tell I don't like him.
Me: Be nice.
12yo: He wears Crocs.
Me: Burn his house down.

— KC of TX (@KCMoore51)

"The PTA needs help with Secret Santa this ye..."

instantly deletes email

— Sarah del Rio (@Est1975Blog)

**I've never been to a yoga class,
but I've taken 30 minutes to exit a baby's
room in slow motion ... so I think I've
done all the positions.**

— The ParentNormal (@ParentNormal)

I've discovered the key to always having a hot cup of coffee!

Never have children.

— Bethany Thies (@BPMBadassMama)

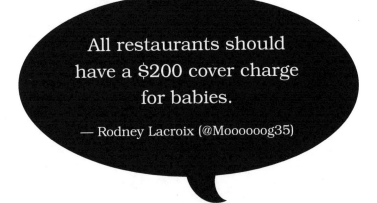

All restaurants should have a $200 cover charge for babies.

— Rodney Lacroix (@Mooooog35)

My little son says "Dark Vader." My melted dad heart is conflicted with my wincing inner nerd about this.

— Andy Herald (@AndyHerald)

No better reminder that you have enough children than going to a kids movie on a holiday weekend.

— Designer Daddy (@DesignerDaddy)

Alligator wrestlers

Contortionists

Professional negotiators

— People most qualified to get a toddler into a sleeper

— Paige Kellerman (@PaigeKellerman)

I'm so glad we have a room full of furniture so that my kids can sit on top of me.

— Jen Good (@BuriedWithKids)

The sounds of my kids arguing over the icing is really turning this gingerbread house into a gingerbread home.

— Simon Holland (@SimonCHolland)

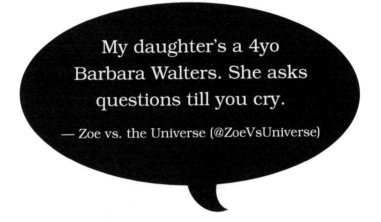

My daughter's a 4yo Barbara Walters. She asks questions till you cry.

— Zoe vs. the Universe (@ZoeVsUniverse)

I passed the stage of parenting where I teach them stuff. Now I just yell at them for not doing the stuff I already taught them how to do.

— Linda Doty (@LindaInDisguise)

My kids don't always cough in my mouth,
but when they do, they have a contagious
viral infection, and I have big plans
three to seven days in the future.

— Kim Bongiorno (@LetMeStart)

Me: What do you want on your burger?

4yo: No mustard. No cheese. No onion. No lettuce. No meat.

Me: So a ketchup sandwich?

4yo: Right.

— Paige Kellerman (@PaigeKellerman)

"Come on, Mom. Just a little bit to calm me down? I just need a little. Please? PLEASE!!!" It seems my son is detoxing from television.

— Outmanned Mommy (@MaryWiddicks)

3yo: What's wrong, Mom?

Me: I don't feel great today.

Deli guy: Can I help you, ma'am?

3yo: MAYBE YOU JUST HAVE TO POOP!

Me: No, that will be all.

— Jennifer Lizza (@OutsmartedMommy)

I'm sorry, he never acts like this. He must be coming down with something.
— Me, lying

— Lurk @ Home Mom (@LurkAtHomeMom)

2yo: I don't want to eat my pork chop!
Me: Name one thing that's wrong with it.
2yo: It's not pizza.
Touché.

— Exploding Unicorn (@XplodingUnicorn)

I'm not sure
our six minutes of playing
in the snow were worth the
forty-five minutes of preparation.
— Stella G. Maddox (@StellaGMaddox)

Humans are weird. Kids lose teeth, and we all celebrate with fairies who exchange money for used bones.

— Nicole Leigh Shaw (@NicoleLeighShaw)

I don't have children;
I have hecklers.

— Andrea (@SheepAndRobots)

"How was hockey? Did you find a cup small enough to cover your weiner?"
— My mother, obliviously giving my son a complex

— Stephanie Jankowski (@CrazyExhaustion)

5yo: I think Santa put me on the naughty list.

Me: What did you do?

5yo: That's between me and Santa.

— La Vie En Meh (@TheAlexNevil)

Ugh, don't even talk to me until I've unravelled a roll of toilet paper, emptied three cabinets and coated the floor in Kix crumbs.

— 1yos

— Lurk @ Home Mom (@LurkAtHomeMom)

4yo: Can we stop at the bakery?

Me: I'm late for work.

4yo: Is work more important than doughnuts?

Me:

4yo:

Me: *stops for doughnuts*

— Exploding Unicorn (@XplodingUnicorn)

Stack of towels? Check.

Two yards of tarp. Check.

Four sets of goggles. Check.

Ok, I'm ready to serve hot cocoa to the kids.

— Paige Kellerman (@PaigeKellerman)

Don't ask your 5yo to feed the cat unless you're sure the cat likes blueberry Pop-Tarts. Lesson learned.

— Stella G. Maddox (@StellaGMaddox)

FADE IN: KITCHEN

A toddler struggles to choose a cup.

Dad: Why is this so hard?

CUT TO: LIVING ROOM

Dad takes four hours to pick Netflix show.

— The ParentNormal (@ParentNormal)

**Slippers made out of Lego
so that when you step on a Lego
you just get taller.**

— Kalvin MacLeod (@KalvinMacLeod)

Yes, Child, I realize that I'm asking you to clean up a mess you didn't make. Just martyr yourself and do it. I'll get word to the Pope.

— QwertyGirl (@QwertyGirl)

My 7yo son walked in on me taking a bath, looked at me for a split second, and then said: "How about we close this curtain?"

— Sarah del Rio (@Est1975Blog)

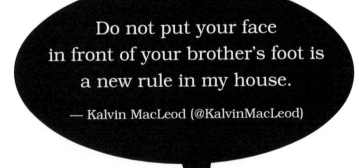

Do not put your face in front of your brother's foot is a new rule in my house.

— Kalvin MacLeod (@KalvinMacLeod)

No, Honey. The deer is just sleeping. They tied him down so he wouldn't fall off the top of their Ford Explorer.

— Linda Doty (@LindaInDisguise)

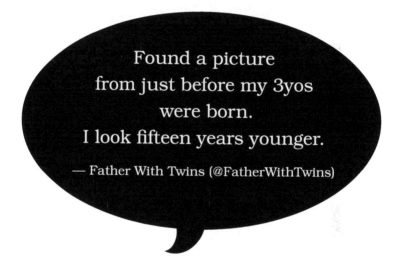

Found a picture
from just before my 3yos
were born.
I look fifteen years younger.

— Father With Twins (@FatherWithTwins)

For a Super Powered Ranger Jedi Master, my son loses his mind pretty easily over a sock being slightly off-center.

— Designer Daddy (@DesignerDaddy)

7yo has been memorizing "The Night Before Christmas." Changed a line to "Threw up on the shutters and grew a mustache." Paternity confirmed.

The Story Behind the Tweet:

There is a magical point in every young reader's development when they switch from wanting you to read to them, to them wanting to read to you. It's the most wonderful thing, because you don't even have to listen. My youngest reached this point just in time to start reading "The Night Before Christmas." I was listening (okay, napping) as she read. And then she made the joke. She stopped just to make sure I caught it, looking up to raise an eyebrow. She's going to be huge in vaudeville someday.

— α geek (@AlfaGeeek)

I tell my kids
to go wash their hands
but they hear, "Go recreate a
scene from *Titanic.*"

— Jennifer Lizza (@OutsmartedMommy)

I've realized I can only keep a finite number of things alive at one time. When I found out I was pregnant, I threw away my houseplants.

— Outmanned Mommy (@MaryWiddicks)

Obviously you need a break when you stare at a pile of unmatched socks and think: Does it makes sense to reference these in my suicide note?

— Andrea (@SheepAndRobots)

6yo: I have two weeks off.

Hairdresser: What are you going to do for two whole weeks?

6yo: After Christmas, probably fight my brother.

— TchrQuotes (@TchrQuotes)

I'm into laughing, not sleeping and rubbing my dinner in my hair. Call my mom for play-date info.
— My toddler on Match.com

— It's Really 10 Months (@Really10Months)

Me: Put on a hat so we can leave for school.

3yo: I don't need a hat; my brain is warm.

Me: My brain is fried and I'm wearing one.

3yo: *puts on hat*

— Jennifer Lizza (@OutsmartedMommy)

Crazy how the only time my kids ever
actually want to talk to me is when it's
through a one-inch crack at the bottom
of the bathroom door.

— Abe Yospe (@Cheeseboy22)

4yo: Can I sleep in your bed? I had a nightmare.
Me: Was it a dream about spending an entire night in your own bed?

— The ParentNormal (@ParentNormal)

Gave the 3yo a sick bell. Let's discuss what a moron I am.

The Story Behind the Tweet:

Last year, when my three-year-old caught the flu, I got the brilliant idea to make her comfortable in my bed on the second floor of our home. And then I gave her a sick bell so she could call me when she needed something important.

That's when I realized that my daughter and I had very different interpretations of the word "important." Important to me was a request for more juice or imminent barfing. Know what a three-year-old thinks is important? The color pink. Bubble Guppies. Sparkly sparkles that sparkle. Grandma.

I'd expected the faint occasional tinkling of her bell. What I got was like nonstop clanging of church bells on a feast day. I see a "lost" bell in my future.

— Stephanie Jankowski (@CrazyExhaustion)

I've been carrying an acorn in my pocket for three months; I never know when my son might want it back, and I want to avoid a meltdown.

— Dad and Buried (@DadAndBuried)

I can't find my kid's birth certificate, but I apparently saved one for every Build-A-Bear we own in a special file because I'm insane.

— Stella G. Maddox (@StellaGMaddox)

It was
COLONEL MUSTARD in the
CHATROOM with the
BULLYING.

— McSweatervest (@McSwtrvst)

New house rule: hide the Lady Remington from the kids.

Especially the kid with only one remaining eyebrow.

— Leslie Marinelli (@TheBeardedIris)

Since becoming parents, the thing my wife and I do most often naked is fall asleep while discussing the possibility of sex.

— Steve Olivas (@SteveOlivas)

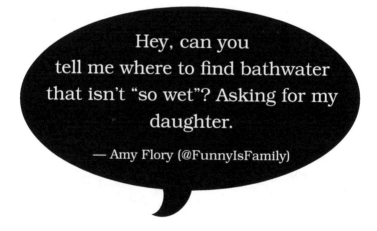

Hey, can you tell me where to find bathwater that isn't "so wet"? Asking for my daughter.

— Amy Flory (@FunnyIsFamily)

I tried to help by doing my daughter's hair, and a kind old lady offered her a hot meal and a warm place to sleep.

— Simon Holland (@SimonCHolland)

I'm glad the young me, the one filled with hopes and dreams, can't see the current me watching a marathon of *Wizards of Waverly Place.*

— Linda Doty (@LindaInDisguise)

The dream is sleeping in on Sunday, the reality is that the sibling rivalry cage match happening in the living room needs a referee.

— Simon Holland (@SimonCHolland)

I don't believe in spanking my children, but I do believe in flipping them off from the other room.

— Jewel Nunez (@OneFunnyMummy)

decorated cookies with 6yo

Me: Go give one to Daddy.

2 hours later

Him: Hey, question. Was that cookie

decorated when you sent it to me?

— MommaUnfiltered (@MommaUnfiltered)

Glossary

It's challenging to squeeze comedic brilliance into Twitter's regulation 140 characters. And when every letter (and space) counts, you need some shortcuts. Welcome to the sub-language of Twitter.

You may recognize some of these mysterious acronyms and abbreviations from scrolling through your tween's or teen's texts or research papers. Some are easy enough to unravel: TY = thank you and YW = you're welcome. But others are impossible to figure out. To that end, we offer this handy guide to Twitter's most commonly used terms and tweet abbreviations. You're welcome.

AFAIK: As far as I know. In other words, "I have no idea, but I simply MUST chime in."

Avi: The image you choose to represent yourself on Twitter. Everyone starts out as an egg. Don't stay an egg.

Bio: Words you choose to describe yourself on Twitter. Must be 160 characters or less.

DM: Direct message. Users can send people who follow them direct messages that will not appear in their public stream. Ask permission before sending, some users are vehemently opposed to DMs because they can be spam vehicles, or because they are far too awesome to be communicated with directly.

Favstar: An online service that tracks the most recent and most popular tweets (based on stars/ retweets). If you become a paying member, each day you can grant your favorite tweet a virtual trophy. Commonly used by Twitter comedians.

FF: Friend Follower/Follow Friday. Often you'll see #FF followed by one or more Twitter handles to follow. This can be irritating when a person has long strings of #FF tweets and they #FF the same tweeps every week.

FML: F--- my life. Often paired with domestic catastrophes: "3yo just poured herself a glass of milk. All over the couch. FML."

FWIW: For what it's worth. Often paired with IMHO. Synonymous with "I am a know-it-all."

Handle: A person's Twitter username. It's how you're identified on Twitter and always follows an @ symbol. What's your Twitter handle, good buddy?

Hashtag: # is a hashtag. Hashtags are used to group tweets by topic for easy search and discovery. For example, if you searched for "#naptime," it would display every tweet using that hashtag. Hashtags are also used as a "kicker" or the punchline to a joke or statement: #That'sWhatSheSaid, for example. Some people use the word "hashtag" in actual conversation, which is ridiculous.

IDGAF: I don't give a f---. Typically added on to the end of a comment. "I'll take eleven items into that ten-item lane. IDGAF. #rebel"

IMHO: In my humble opinion. Usage of this term is rarely humble.

IRL: In real life. Commonly used for events or meetings that occur in real time with actual, live humans.

LOL: Laughing out loud. Your mom might think LOL means "lots of love." It does not. Do not allow her to put LOL on sympathy cards.

MT: Modified tweet. Resending an edited version of another's tweet to your followers with proper credit and modification noted. For when the sender just HAS to add their two cents. Many tweeters don't love modified tweets because of their giant egos.

NFW: No f---ing way. As in "There is NFW the 2yo is sleeping in my bed tonight." Spoiler alert: The 2yo is sleeping in your bed tonight.

OH or O/H: Overheard. Example: "O/H from backseat: Boogers aren't gross, boogers are delicious."

RT: Retweet. Retweeting sends an unedited version of another's tweet to your followers with proper credit. Tweeters love retweets because of their giant egos.

Star: Clicking the little star icon is like giving the tweeter a virtual high-five. Many tweeters' entire self-worth is tied up in stars and retweets.

Subtweet: A passive-aggressive tweet directed at another tweep or group of tweeps without mentioning any names. They've been known to cause Twitter Drama. Can also be a nice tweet, but often referred to in a negative manner.

TL: Timeline. Where the tweets happen. Shows every tweet by everyone you follow in real time. Eventually, endlessly scrolling through a TL will give rise to carpal tunnel syndrome.

Twitter comedian: All the contributors to this book. Anyone known on Twitter as a joke-tweeter.

TC: Twitter crush. A crush developed on another tweep based on their avi or because they've given your tweets extra attention via stars or retweets. It's kind of pathetic, but happens. It goes something like this: "Why did my TC RT her and not me?"

ToTD: Tweet of the Day. A virtual trophy bestowed upon a particular tweet by a member of Favstar.

Tweep: A tweeter or person who tweets. It's unclear whether this term is cool or nerdy. Or cool because it's nerdy.

QOTD: Quote of the day. The best or most startling line uttered over the course of a day, "QOTD: Look, Mummy, the baby doesn't even cry when I hit her with this shoe."

YO or yo: Year-old. Used in conjunction with a number to represent a child of that age. For example, "4yo just told me he pooped. In my bed. #KillMeNow"

Contributors

α geek (@AlfaGeeek)

AlfaGeeek.wordpress.com

My wife doesn't think I'm funny. My three kids think I'm hilarious. Odds are, my wife is right.

Hot Breakfast (@AmyDillon)

HotBrkfast.com

Does "mad" apply more to people working in advertising or staying home with their kids? This donut-loving, patience-lacking mom of two boys is finding out.

Andy H. (@AndyAsAdjective)

Father to two girls; husband to a patient wife; lover of Twitter comedy; runner, writer and reformed breakfast-cereal addict.

Andy Herald (@AndyHerald)

HowToBeADad.com

Humorist, designer, owner of a beard and father to three sons. You will know him by his earbuds. Also, his youngest son glued the shift key on his laptop.

Bethany Thies (@BPMBadassMama)

BadParentingMoments.com

"THAT lady" *eyebrow raised* with the screaming kids is me. Nice to meet you.

Brad Broaddus (@BradBroaddus)

Father to four crazy kids. He spends most of his time chasing kids and wondering why he didn't just get a dog.

Jen Good (@BuriedWithKids)

The doctor said, "There's two and something else." I said, "Dear God, let it be a tumor." Then I became the proud mom to triplets and their big brother.

Abe Yospe (@Cheeseboy22)

I type words on my home computer and then, using an Internet connection, I post those words to the World Wide Web. In my spare time, I teach first grade.

Stephanie Jankowski (@CrazyExhaustion)

WhenCrazyMeetsExhaustion.com

English teacher by trade, smack talker by nature, Stephanie is a mother of three who lives by the mantra: Life is too short! Laugh!

Mike Julianelle (@DadAndBuried)

DadAndBuried.com

A thirtysomething Brooklynite who is sharing his experiences as a father and bitching about the ways the existence of his son is destroying his social life.

Brent Almond (@DesignerDaddy)

DesignerDaddy.com

Comics-loving, work-at-home graphic designer/ blogger and forty-five-year-old gay dad of a five-year-old son. Utility belt contents: Starbucks, Advil, Just for Men.

Domestic Goddess (@DomesticGoddss)

UnderachievingDomesticGoddess.blogspot.com

I'm a fifty percenter giving seventy-five percent! Mom of three boys trying to raise three good men who put the toilet seat down. Professional giggler and philanthropist extraordinaire.

Sarah del Rio (@Est1975Blog)

Established1975.com

Mother of one. Grower of chin hairs. Leaker of pee. One foot in grave. Writer and editor. Writer of the humor blog est. 1975, for the ladies of Generation X.

Father With Twins (@FatherWithTwins)

When I'm not building business strategies, I'm playing with my five-year-olds, watching sports, or annoying my wife. Hmm, those last two are synonymous.

Chrissy Howe (@FullMetalMommy)

FullMetalMommy.com

Fearless, ever-pregnant mother warrior to three little hand grenades. I share my life like an open book, but keep your grubby mitts off of my chocolate.

Amy Flory (@FunnyIsFamily)

FunnyIsFamily.com

Named one of Mashable's 17 Funny Moms on Twitter in 2013 and Year's Meanest Mom by her kids in 2015.

Housewife of Hell (@HousewifeOfHell)

Worst housewife ever. Mother to mortified teenage twins. Freelancer for Anne Taintor, Inc. Hobbies include tweeting and napping. Also known as Ellen Macdonald.

Kalvin MacLeod (@KalvinMacLeod)

I don't know what I'm doing.

Kate Hall (@KateWhineHall)

HallofTweets.com

Stay-at-home mom of three kids. When I'm not answering bizarre questions or wiping poop off the walls, you can find me on Twitter.

KC of TX (@KCMoore51)

Husband, father, proud Texan, Twitter addict and enthusiast of any and all things related to tacos, yoga pants, pillow forts, and Oreos.

Kim Bongiorno (@LetMeStart)

LetMeStartBySayingBlog.com

Mom, wife, author, blogger, freelance writer. If she were less tired, she'd totally jazz up her bio so you'd never forget this moment.

Linda Doty (@LindainDisguise)

JustLinda.com

A mom since '83, Linda's got a decade before her fifth daughter is grown. She hopes to be discovered but is worried it'll be by a concerned mental health worker.

Contributors

Lurk @ Home Mom (@LurkAtHomeMom)

You'll see me. I'll be the mom in line for the family bathroom in the mall with tiny ketchup handprints all over my shirt.

Marlene (@MarleBean)

Quirky mom of two silly kids and one big kid/husband. Juggling it all with sass and class. But if anyone asks, I'm writing these jokes for a Pinterest project.

Mary Widdicks (@MaryWiddicks)

OutmannedMommy.com

My husband calls me Honey. My sons call me Mommy. The baby calls me Milk. The dogs call me their indentured servant. I am a writer and a SAHM. I am outmanned.

Wendy S. (@MaughamMom)

Minivan mom. Probably an unwitting accomplice to my kids' plans for world domination. I never turn down dessert.

Carisa Miller (@MCarisa)

CarisaMiller.com

Forever adjusting my undergarments in public. Writer, director, humorist, nut job. Wife of my husband. Mother of two fireball daughters and an ill-tempered cat.

McSweatervest (@McSwtrvst)

Yes, I do wear sweatervests. And somehow I still became a parent. There's hope, nerds.

Linda Roy (@ModMomElleroy)

ElleroyWasHere.com

Lives in New Jersey with her husband and two boys, who say she's the female Larry David. She'll criticize your parallel parking to prove it. She blogs and tweets and curates her son's booger collection.

Rodney Lacroix (@Moooooog35)

RodneyLacroix.com

Best-selling, award-winning author of humor and comedy books. Father. Husband. Amazing lover. Vertically challenged and very, very lazy.

MommaUnfiltered (@MommaUnfiltered)

As the mother of a nineteen-, a nine-, and a six-year-old, I'm uniquely qualified to say kids suck at any age.

Deva Dalporto (@MyLifeSuckers)

MyLifeSuckers.com

When she's not making parody videos and singing about her saggy boobs on YouTube, Deva is busy trying to prevent her two kids from slaughtering each other.

Nicole Leigh Shaw (@NicoleLeighShaw)

NicoleLeighShaw.com

All four of my kids are still breathing. Award, please. I blog at NicoleLeighShaw.com where I've embarrassed my mother many, many times.

Creed (@NoviceFather)

DadForBeginners.com

Dad to son. Husband to wife. Enemy to few. Friend to fewer. Indifferent to most. I only shave once a week. I once killed a spider with my bare hands. I'm a carnivore and my wife is vegan, so basically I suffer a lot.

Jewel Nunez (@OneFunnyMummy)

OneFunnyMummy.com

One Funny Mummy writes what she knows: chaos and poop. She lives in Whine Country with her funny hubby, two cheeky monkeys and her dwindling sanity.

Jennifer Lizza (@OutsmartedMommy)

OutsmartedMommy.com

Mom of two energy-filled, lovable boys. Traded in my salary to raise them. They outsmart me daily. It's probably the lack of sleep.

Paige Kellerman (@PaigeKellerman)

PaigeKellerman.com

Writer, humorist and mother. People say I'm a bad cook. They're right. Author of the book *At Least My Belly Hides My Cankles*.

Chris Cate (@ParentNormal)

ParentNormal.com

A three-time parent, all-time minivan driver, no-time sleeper and The ParentNormal author, trying to stay awake long enough to turn his tweets into books.

Pete Lynch (@PJTLynch)

Along with raising three boys, Pete spends his remaining time on the Internets, writing comedy and pretending to run Long John Silver's.

Amanda Mushro (@QuestionableCIP)

QuestionableChoicesInParenting.com

Candy Land loser, yoga pants enthusiast, and mom of two who's laughing at life as a parent so they don't commit her.

Tracy (@QwertyGirl)

OrangeAndSilverBlog.blogspot.com

Tracy fills her days helping her kids find their stuff, figuring out what's for dinner, and repeating that "socks without feet in them do not belong in the living room."

Celeste, Kim and Natalie (@Really10Months)

ItsReally10Months.com

Delivering the truth about pregnancy, parenting and the randomness of life. Authors of the book *It's Really 10 Months*.

Sarcastic Mommy (@SarcasticMommy4)

Trying to be queen of an all-male household with a husband, four boys and a male dog. My life is … interesting.

Andrea (@SheepAndRobots)

Single, career mom looking after two boys and my dad. To fully accept living with all males, I now douse myself with asparagus urine and lean into a sneeze.

Simon Holland (@SimonCHolland)

SweetAndWeak.com

If Hollywood made a movie about my life, the actor playing me would be whoever is best at walking around their house turning off lights.

Stella G. Maddox (@StellaGMaddox)

StellaMaddox.com

Recovering stay-at-home mom. You can usually find her hiding in the bathroom since she doesn't play well with others.

Steve Olivas (@SteveOlivas)

Air drummer in the Twitter garage band, playing gigs when my wife lets me. Please hold your applause until after the kids move out.

Keith Newbery (@TchrQuotes)

Keith is a husband and father from Kansas. He has three kids and a dog. When he's not exploiting his children on Twitter, he is a high school English teacher.

La Vie En Meh (@TheAlexNevil)

Alex ot his big break playing "Daddy" and can now be seen in *NO NO NO!* and *Fine, Here's Some Candy*. His child is occasionally cute.

Leslie Marinelli (@TheBeardedIris)

LeslieMarinelli.com

Humorist, editor, and invisible vessel for grandchildren and PTA donations since 1999.

Lauren (@WorkingMom86)

An exhausted working mom of an energetic toddler, she shares excerpts of her gradual descent into madness.

Exploding Unicorn (@XplodingUnicorn)

I'm an upstanding human being, except for when I'm not, which is almost always.

Yuvi Zalkow (@YuviZalkow)

YuviZalkow.com

Dad, husband, novelist, podcaster, essayist, tweeter, grocery store shopper, hider in the bathroom, weeper under the desk, stasher of vodka. Bald.

E. R. Catalano (@ZoeVsUniverse)

ZoeVsTheUniverse.com

Mother to an evil mastermind-in-training.
Amateur at life. Professional at the laugh-cry.

*You can read in-depth interviews with many
of our contributors at HallOfTweets.com.*

Acknowledgments

Many thanks to:

Our contributors. The most hilarious group of parents to nab a Twitter handle. Without you, this book wouldn't exist. Or it might, but it would be REALLY short. Like five pages. We've enjoyed getting to know each of you—you're all hilarious. Thank you for making us laugh.

Jeff Terry of JeffAndJillWentUpTheHill.com. For always coming back for more. Your help in selecting tweets for this book, the first book, as well as monthly on Kate's Hall of Tweets has been invaluable. That you would be honored to be part of our projects humbles us all. We can't wait to meet you in person some day!

Linda Doty (@LindaInDisguise). Not only did you make us laugh with your tweet contributions, but you helped us select the funniest of the funny. Thank you for your hard work.

Roz Warren. For your amazing ability to get our first book out there and seen by so many, to you we owe one million thanks.

Farah Miller and Emma Mustich of *The Huffington Post.* Thank you for contributing the foreword to this book and for consistently finding the funniest parenting tweets, week in and week out. The tweeps appreciate it, and your selections make the whole world laugh.

Nicole Leigh Shaw. Thank you for your eagle-eyes and the loving care you took proofing our book. You saved us all from looking ridiculous. And we're grateful.

Our husbands. For your support and encouragement and for learning during the production of Book One that the best course of action is to take the kids far, far away when we are in crunch mode.

Our kids: Sheehan, Josiah, Autumn, Holden and Fletcher. For laughing at the tweets and illustrations in our first book, even when you didn't always "get it." Someday it will all make perfect sense.

Every follower who reads, stars and retweets our contributors' funny tweets. Without you we wouldn't be here. You keep us coming back to launch our funny into the Twitterverse. Well, you, and our enormous egos. But mostly you.

All the Twitter comedians, parents or otherwise. Thank you ALL for making us laugh every day.

Twitter. Thank you for giving us the challenge of a 140 character-platform to share our funny. Thanks for letting our voices be heard, especially those of us who are introverts.

About the Editors

Kate Hall

If anyone's looking for Kate Hall, check Twitter first. That's where you'll usually find her. She loves Twitter so much that she created a blog, *Hall of Tweets*, devoted entirely to—you guessed it!—Twitter. Besides her Top 10 Funniest Tweets lists, she conducts "Beyond the Bio" interviews, giving fans a "behind the tweets" peek at their favorite Twitter comedians.

Named one of the 100 Top Twitter Users in Chicago, Kate also routinely makes HuffPost Parent's Funniest Parenting Tweets of the Week. Her tweets are regularly featured on Modern Mom and NickMom.

When not on Twitter or writing about Twitter, Kate blogs at *Can I Get Another Bottle of Whine?*, where she writes laugh-out-loud stories about the reality of life. Her essays have also appeared on *Chicago Parent* and *The Huffington Post* and in *The HerStories Project* anthology. Kate was the co-editor and all-around tweep-wrangler for *The Big Book of Parenting Tweets*, published in 2014.

Norine Dworkin-McDaniel & Jessica Ziegler are the co-creators of Science of Parenthood. An illustrated humor blog that uses faux math and snarky science to "explain" baffling parenting situations, Science of Parenthood was named one of Parenting.com's "blogs every parent should read."

The Big Book of Parenting Tweets was Jessica's brain baby, and, as per their partnership agreement requiring support of each other's lunatic schemes, Norine happily co-developed and co-edited the book.

When not pretending to "get" Twitter, Norine and Jessica are busy writing and illustrating their upcoming book *Science of Parenthood: Thoroughly Unscientific Explanations for Utterly Baffling Parenting Situations*, coming November 2015 from She Writes Press.

Want more?

Check out the hilarious book
that started it all,
The Big Book of Parenting Tweets
available on Amazon.com and
BarnesandNoble.com

More than 70 5-star Amazon reviews!

If you enjoyed this book, please consider leaving a rating on Amazon or Goodreads.com,

It helps indie publishers tremendously, and we truly appreciate it!

THANK YOU!

Learn more about this book, the first volume, *The Big Book of Parenting Tweets*, our contributors and upcoming volumes at BigBookOfTweets.com

———————

The Big Book of Parenting Tweets
and *The Bigger Book of Parenting Tweets*
were created by Science of Parenthood.
Visit ScienceOfParenthood.com to learn more.

Made in the USA
San Bernardino, CA
08 June 2015